CHAOTIC ANGELS

Gwyneth Lewis was Wales's National Poet from 2005 to 2006, the first writer to be given the Welsh laureateship. Her first six books of poetry in Welsh and English were followed by *Chaotic Angels* (Bloodaxe Books, 2005), which brings together the poems from her three English collections, *Parables & Faxes*, *Zero Gravity* and *Keeping Mum*. Her latest poetry books are *A Hospital Odyssey* (2010) and *Sparrow Tree* (2011), both from Bloodaxe.

Her first collection in English, *Parables & Faxes* (Bloodaxe Books, 1995), won the Aldeburgh Poetry Festival Prize and was shortlisted for the Forward Prize for Best First Collection. Her second, *Zero Gravity* (Bloodaxe Books, 1998), was shortlisted for the Forward Prize for Poetry. The BBC made a documentary of *Zero Gravity*, inspired by her astronaut cousin's voyage to repair the Hubble Space Telescope. Both *Zero Gravity* and *Keeping Mum* (Bloodaxe Books, 2003) were Poetry Book Society Recommendations. *Y Llofrudd Iaith* (Barddas, 1999) won the Welsh Arts Council Book of the Year Prize and *Keeping Mum* was shortlisted for the same prize. In 2010 she won a Cholmondeley Award. *Sparrow Tree* won the Roland Mathias Poetry Award (Wales Book of the Year) in 2012. She gave the Newcastle/Bloodaxe Poetry Lectures in 2014, *Quantum Poetics*, published by Bloodaxe.

Gwyneth Lewis composed the words on the front of Cardiff's Wales Millennium Centre. Her other books include *Sunbathing in the Rain: A Cheerful Book on Depression* (Harper Perennial, 2002), shortlisted for the Mind Book of the Year; *Two in a Boat* (Fourth Estate, 2005), which recounts a voyage made with her husband on a small boat from Cardiff to North Africa; and *The Meat Tree: New stories from the Mabinogion* (Seren, 2010).

She is a librettist and has written two chamber operas for children, *Redflight/Barcud*, with music by Richard Chew, and *Dolffin*, with music by Julian Phillips. She has also written an oratorio, *The Most Beautiful Man from the Sea*, to music by Orlando Gough and Richard Chew. Her first stage play, *Clytemnestra*, was premièred at Sherman Cymru in 2012.

Gwyneth Lewis
CHAOTIC ANGELS

POEMS IN ENGLISH

BLOODAXE BOOKS

ISBN: 978 1 85224 723 2

First published 2005 by
Bloodaxe Books Ltd,
Eastburn,
South Park
Hexham,
Northumberland NE46 1BS.

www.bloodaxebooks.com
For further information about Bloodaxe titles
please visit our website and join our mailing list
or write to the above address for a catalogue.

Supported using public funding by
**ARTS COUNCIL
ENGLAND**

This is a digital reprint of the 2005 edition.

CONTENTS

ACKNOWLEDGEMENTS

This book includes all the poems from Gwyneth Lewis's first three Bloodaxe collections *Parables & Faxes* (1995), *Zero Gravity* (1998) and *Keeping Mum* (2003). It excludes her later titles *A Hospital Odyssey* (2010) and *Sparrow Tree* (2011).

Parables & Faxes: *Welsh Espionage* was first published in *Poetry Review*, and four poems from the sequence appeared in the first edition of *Parables & Faxes* (1995). The full version was restored for the second impression (1997) and for this edition.

Zero Gravity: *The Mind Museum* was commissioned by Fiet and, as *Museum of the Air*, was set to music by John Metcalf. The work was first performed by the BBC National Orchestra of Wales at St David's Hall in Cardiff on 29 March 1998. The version published here is slightly revised. The opening of 'Soul Candles' is based on a line from Thomas Traherne. The first two lines of 'Will and the Wall' are the translation of a Welsh saying. The epigraph to *Zero Gravity* is from *Space Facts* by Caroline Stott and Clint Twist (Dorling Kindersley, 1995); the quotation is taken from page 13.

Keeping Mum: I would like to acknowledge Barddas, publisher of *Y Llofrudd Iaith* in 1999 and Richard Poole for his translation of 'Her End'. I'm grateful to the City of London Festival for permission to publish *Chaotic Angels*, poems commissioned for the Angel Series of concerts in 2002.

I am extremely grateful to NESTA for its support. The National Endowment for Science, Technology and the Arts awarded me a five-year fellowship in 2001.

This book is dedicated to Leighton.

PARABLES & FAXES

(1995)

Pentecost

The Lord wants me to go to Florida.
I shall cross the border with the mercury thieves,
as foretold in the faxes and prophecies,
and the checkpoint angel of Estonia
will have alerted the uniformed birds
to act unnatural and distract the guards

so I pass unhindered. My glossolalia
shall be my passport – I shall taste the tang
of travel on the atlas of my tongue –
salt Poland, sour Denmark and sweet Vienna
and all men in the Spirit shall understand
that, in His wisdom, the Lord has sent

a slip of a girl to save great Florida.
I shall tear through Europe like a standing flame,
not pausing for long, except to rename
the occasional city; in Sofia
thousands converted and hundreds slain
in the Holy Spirit along the Seine.

My life is your chronicle; O Florida
revived, look forward to your past,
and prepare your perpetual Pentecost
of golf course and freeway, shopping mall and car
so the fires that are burning in the orange groves
turn light into sweetness and the huddled graves

are the hives of the future – an America
spelt plainly, translated in the Everglades
where palm fruit hang like hand grenades
ready to rip whole treatises of air.
Then the S in the tail of the crocodile
will make perfect sense to the bibliophile

who will study this land, his second Torah.
All this was revealed. Now I wait for the Lord
to move heaven and earth to send me abroad
and fulfil His bold promise to Florida.
As I stay put, He shifts His continent:
Atlantic closes, the sheet of time is rent.

The Hedge

With hindsight, of course, I can see that the hedge
was never my cleverest idea
and that bottles of vodka are better not wedged

like fruit in its branches, to counter fears
and shakes in the morning on the way to work.
Looking back, I can see how I pushed it too far

when I'd stop in the lay-by for a little lurk
before plunging my torso in, shoulder high
to the hedgerow's merciful root-and-branch murk

till I'd felt out my flattie and could drink in the dry
and regain my composure with the cuckoo-spit.
Then, with growing wonder, I'd watch the fungi,

lovely as coral in the aqueous light.
Lovely, that is, till that terrible day
when the hedge was empty. Weakened by fright

I leant in much deeper to feel out which way
the bottle had rolled and, cursing my luck
(hearing already what my bosses would say

about my being caught in this rural ruck),
I started to panic, so I tussled and heaved
and tried to stand upright, but found I was stuck.

I struggled still harder, but you'd scarcely believe
the strength in a hedge that has set its mind
on holding a person in its vice of leaves

and this one was proving a real bind.
With a massive effort, I took the full strain
and tore up the hedgerow, which I flicked up behind

me, heavy and formal as a wedding train.
I turned and saw, to my embarrassment,
that I'd pulled up a county with my new-found mane,

11

which was still round my shoulders, with its tell-tale scent
of loam and detritus, while trunk roads and streams
hung off me like ribbons. It felt magnificent:

minerals hidden in unworked seams
shone like slub silver in my churned-up trail.
I had brooches of newly built housing schemes

and sequins of coruscating shale;
power-lines crackled as they changed their course
and woodsmoke covered my face like a veil.

Only then did I feel the first pangs of remorse.
Still, nobody'd noticed so, quickly, I knelt,
took hold of the landscape, folded and forced

it up to a chignon which I tied with my belt.
It stayed there, precarious. The occasional spray
of blackthorn worked loose, but I quickly rebuilt

the ropey construction and tucked it away.
Since then I've become quite hard to approach:
I chew mints to cover the smell of decay

which is with me always. Food tastes of beech
and I find that I have to concentrate
on just holding the hairstyle since it's started to itch

and the people inside it are restless of late.
Still, my tresses have won me a kind of renown
for flair and I find my hair titillates

certain men who want me to take it down
in front of them, slowly. But with deepening dread
I'm watching my old self being overgrown

while scruples rustle like quadrupeds,
stoat-eyed, sharp-toothed in my tangled roots
(it's so hard to be human with a hedge on your head!).

Watch me. Any day I'll be bearing fruit,
sweet hips that glint like pinpricks of blood
and my dry land drowning will look quite cute

to those who've never fallen foul of wood.
But on bad days now I see nothing but hedge,
my world crazed by the branches of should,

for I've lost all centre, have become an edge
and though I wear my pearls like dew
I feel that I've paid for my sacrilege

as I wish for my autumn with its broader view.
But for now I submit. With me it will die,
this narrowness, this slowly closing eye.

The Voledom of Skomer

For thirty years a suburban naturalist
has studied the life of the SKOMER VOLE
as a pattern of *rodent parochial*.
His colleagues consider him a purist,
look down on his subject as insular,
but he's entranced by the phenomena of local
and all things SKOMER are his exotica.

He's made a fetish of specificity:
the Ramsey field vole's all very well
and yes, he quite likes the pipistrelle,
but the SKOMER VOLE? – Passionate loyalty
and an endless interest in the ins and outs
of a vole that is wholly residual,
one that missed, as it were, the mainland boat

and, surrounded by water, took a snack and just stayed.
In secret he cherishes a mythic version:
the Ur-Vole, a Moses, leads an excursion
across the causeway on a vole crusade
down the slopes of the slippery Continental Shelf
to Skomer to visionary seclusion,
and the safety of his supernatural self.

In the field he's a hawk-eyed devotee,
finding births, deaths and couplings a revelation,
for one man's life spans many generations
of SKOMER VOLE nations and dynasties.
He stoops like a question while, above him, the sky
tries in vain to touch his imagination;
clouds on their columns of rain pass him by,

for he's not drawn to the world by grandeur
but by hours of waiting for the flash of a tail,
for that blur in the dune grass that might be a male.
No, he's wooed through his voleish sense of wonder,
tied by attention to a piece of land
that he feels, one evening, might just set sail
for its observant and most loving husband.

Illinois Idylls

No idyll's reached
without the gravest
difficulty.

1

The Boeing dreams its boarding passengers
which are poured, like poison, through its weeping ear.

Jet mushrooms spore their speed in troposphere,
staining the skies above the glacier

where evening's amber and the sea wind blurs
the iceberg galaxies. A drinker stirs

her cocktail and gulps down her time.
Nothing she sees around her can redeem

the tawdry earrings of her whiskey tears,
for she is addicted to the 'over there',

flies blind through high cathedrals
while, below, a city's bar chart reappears:

a human experiment in scrapers' stairs,
temples, ziggurats. Results Not Known.

She has drunk the compass, but its north swings home
and the bride in her veil of Ativan

grows lovelier as the ground draws near
for she is contracted to vertiginous air,

that is, till the runway's shattered shear
shall make her walk out the shining shards of here.

Even the sorrowful
must practise
weeping.

2 *The Correctional Centre*

sets out to make our refractions straight.
Its corridors of bevelled glass
take, like water, the inmates' weight,
for each of us lives by a different gravity.

The building ripples. Liquid hexagons
lap and unloop along pallid walls.
Legs bend mid-muscle. The Centre's halls
are submerged in institutional remorse.

We wade through wisdom. Herons take flight
when we startle them with the boiler room light
and its mangrove sweetness. This new element
is love's surprising geometry

for we are reformed of our rectitude
(of that tree at A-2, that bird at B-3)
and are fully committed to curvature
so that when, at last, we're let out of here

we'll see the world buckle and the highway's rod
ruck to infinity, for buoyancy
has made pliant my spirit. And when I observe
the cats' eyes' blessings, I speed up and then...swerve!

*For love gives
us life in a
different
element...*

3

This summer we got our own turning lane,
which makes coming to visit from Rural Route Six
a good deal less dangerous.
Change gear as you enter. Take in the cool
and golden shimmer of the driveway's trees,
avoiding land turtles, startling the quail.

Outside it's like an aquarium.
We sleep by kind currents of leafy light
while humming birds suckle on all that's sweet
and sapsuckers tap on our window panes,
waking us subtly from dry-land dreams.
No idyll is real without jealousy.

We dive down to breakfast. What others breathe
is to us unfamiliar. All that we need
is time and each other, for we conjugate
our love into children, and their children in turn
call us to danger in the shattering sun
outside, where it takes all our strength not to drown.

... so let us
live out odes
to simplicity.

4 *Homecoming*

Two rivers deepening into one;
less said, more meant; a field of corn
adjusting to harvest; a battle won

by yielding; days emptied to their brim;
an autumn; a wedding; a logarithm;
self-evidence earned, a coming home

to something brand new but always known;
not doing, but being – a single noun;
now in infinity; a fortune found

in all that's disposable; not out there, but in,
the ceremonials of light in the rain;
the power of being nothing, but sane.

Even the wood
pile is whole,
with its
hidden snake.

5

God damn it, it's gone and done it again
and I didn't see it! I was up with the dawn,
hoping to catch the house and the farm

reforming themselves to integrity.
But nothing. Even the shagbark hickory
was back to where it was yesterday

though I saw it melting and being undone
by evening, exploding into the dark and random
disintegration of all daylight's forms

till it lost all its treeness in a whirling roar
that surrounded the kitchen. I don't know how we dare
presume our pathways will always be there

or how we imagine that from day to day
we'll recognise husbands or the Milky Way,
as they're ruined and righted for our ignorant gaze,

pushed through time's twisters and night's tornadoes,
each atom returning to a shape it once knew
and the morning's still rising – at least, for now!

The katydids
still calling
have failed to
find a mate.

6

Once, I went after the whip poor will.
I was tired of hearing such a haunting call
without knowing the caller. So, armed with a torch
I left all the others on the netted porch
and set out in the crackling electric night.

I paused in a clearing. Around me arose
six callers, six fountains, six triangles of song
so lost and alluring they made me long
for myself and for a glimpse of the source
of such ravishing radar, seen face to face.

But whip poor wills are ventriloquists
of distance and difficult to place
in the dark and deciduous paradise
of night, calls falling around me like leaves,
the cicada my beacon, soft moths my eyes.

For each time a bird would call out its name
(as if it knew itself) I'd stumble and slide
towards it, hoping to use the beam
of my torch to locate it and pin it there,
beak open, eye glinting, blind but aware

that it had been seen and was fully known.
But it never happened. I stood alone
and the tracer atoms of the fireflies
prickled my skin as I took my fill
of the absent, still-calling whip poor will.

*All men should
listen for
the wind beneath
the water.*

7

This pond is full to the brim of itself,
with bullfrogs roaring their geiger applause
for nothing much happening; green darner patrols
with their dry-paper whirring; fish in the trees
and the water rippling its repeated breeze
of reflection weather.

From the bank we watch the pond like a prayer
transforming itself: how molecules of air
are forced through the fringes as the water fights
its own plenty with hunger in the calamus
and everything changes to stay the same.
The dogs hush up and watch the dusk with us.

The currents are coloured scarves round our legs –
forget about air, about human words
for, seen through the surface, the trees iridesce.
Swim in communion as the bats swoop down,
as the woods grow closer, brilliant with gloom
to show us, returning, our best way home.

8

This morning I saw two dinosaurs
locked in combat, their silhouette
heraldic as they held their claws
rampant, two cardinals at war
over their seed, their histories.

Dragons are everywhere. They feed
on cicada fountains, suck dry the roots
and etymologies of trees
to a wordless electricity
turned up by heat to the tautest degree.

We live in ignorance: a child
digs in the dirt for mammoth bones
his father has planted while, over the hill
time turns reptilian and the aeons roll
round the turtle's bite down as it kisses its kill.

*O, give us the
strength for the
long journey from
'she' to 'I'.*

9 *Aunt and Uncle*

You two are the good place
where the others come
to celebrate company on the lawn
with illegal fireworks.
Lightning marbles the suburban sky;
Champaign Urbana is far away
and forgotten as the friends sit down
on rugs and deckchairs and dogs run round
sniffing each other.
The show begins and we applaud
the yellow hornets and coloured pearls
that might, any moment, bring the cops –
colours that make the boys' shadows leap
as far as the driveway;
you watching the light,
me watching you,
so happy the chiggers forgot to bite
and mosquitos were silent
as the spirit pushed
all forms of noxiousness
away for a moment;
nearby in the corn
as the moon grew great
and the night like day
a radio sang to itself and the 'coons,
blasting out Big Band
to the Milky Way.

We are spheres
that are forced
to live in a
line.

10 *Hike to the Vine*

First, we all defied gravity
by scaling a toppled hickory
from roots to branches: dogs barked like birds
and we laughed like leaves at the clarity
of the fallen angles and the rotting tree.

Then we crossed the creek and took on space,
crashed through patches of sassafras,
for men, unlike water, take the longest route
to reason, so we ditched all things straight
and sidled our way though the leaf-crazed light

to the vine, where we were ambushed up by time.
The boys climbed up and hung like fruit
and swung, each in turn, like a pendulum
over us adults, weighed down by shadow
and the knowledge that moving clocks run slow.

*Two-thirds water
calls to three-
quarters sea.*

11

Webbed feet run in the family,
skin holds to its tribal memory
of waves and peace in a rising sea.

As babies we float and fall asleep;
where others find water thin and grope
for safety, we trust the deep

and know how to find the water's grain.
Where others flounder, we recline
and find instinctively the line

of least resistance through the river's steel.
We slip inside the current's wheels,
emerge in robes of trailing pearls

till we dive to silence. God of buoyancy,
give us more breath so that we may be
athletes in Your sufficiency.

For truly this
moment is a world
without end.

12

These snapshot idylls shall outlast their weather:
the cousins like gases, re-arranged on the lawn,
inert and reacting, are rhymes to each other
and reason. See the lilac moon,

it's a dress for their mother, should she put it on
and live out the moment of a luna moth
whose sails shall unfurl in the gale-force sun
that will break them. We are words in the mouth

of daylight, we are undone by the dark.
But ride on the present and cousins shall live
in plenitude to the camera's click
which gives its quick blessings to all we receive.

A Golf-Course Resurrection

Mid morning, above the main road's roar
the fairway's splendid – eighteen holes
high on a mountain, which should be all slope,
too steep for a stretch of evenness or poise.
By logic this layout shouldn't work at all
but all the best places are untenable
and the greens are kind as mercy, the course
an airy, open paradox.

The golfers move like penitents,
shouldering bags and counting strokes
towards the justices of handicap and par.
The wind, as sharp as blessing, brings its own tears.
Just out of sight is the mess below:
deconsecrated chapels, the gutted phurnacite,
tips reshaped by crustacean JCBs,
tracts of black bracken that spent the night on fire.

There is a light of last things here.
These men have been translated from the grime
of working the furnace with its sulphur and fire
into primary colours and leisurewear.

They talk of angles, swings and spins.
Their eyes sprout crows' feet as they squint to see
parabolas and arcs, an abstract vision, difficult to learn,
harder to master, but the chosen ones
know what it is to play without the ball
when – white on white – against the Beacons' snow
the point goes missing, yet they carry on
with a sharper focus on their toughest hole,
steer clear of the bunkers, of their own despair,
sinking impossible shots with the softest of putts
still accurate, scoring an albatross
as around them the lark and the kestrel ride
on extravagant fountains of visible air.

Looking for the Celts

The Duchess of Mecklenburg straightens her back,
surveys her fellow enthusiasts,
all digging in soft Salzkammergut rain.
She swaps her mattock for a favourite pick,
glances up at the Hallstatt peak
then, rested, tackles the grave again.

He's close. She can smell him. With trembling hands,
she sorts bone splinters and pottery shards,
sets them aside with the Celtic coins.
She drops to her knees, forgetting her crew,
scrambles, then gives a triumphant cry
as she touches his chest, his barbarian loins.

The Duchess of Mecklenburg, an eminent
archaeologist, was one of those responsible for
excavating the Celtic salt mines in Hallstatt,
Austria, at the turn of this century.

A Soviet Waiter

(for Viveka)

I am a Soviet waiter
with buttocks hard and tight.
I lord it over the populace
from my dictatorial height.

My mercy's a measure of vodka
served with a swish of the hand.
When foreigners get stroppy
I pretend I don't understand.

I'm supremely indifferent to smiling,
I'm scarcity's entrepreneur.
You're demand, I'm supply – so remember
normality's saboteur.

Convenience is my currency,
discomfort my stock-in-trade.
When grown men start to beg for food
I know I've got it made.

The odd benign dictator
slips through our swinging doors,
but it's never long till we move him along
and he's polishing corridor floors.

Forget the ideals of service,
I'm hunger and hope's new tsar.
I may not vote in elections
but I carry the samovar.

I feed on the diners' waiting,
grow fat on their silent rage.
Bugger the boys in the Kremlin,
this is the waiter's age.

[Tallinn, 1989]

29

Six Poems on Nothing

I *Midwinter Marriage*

After autumn's fever and its vivid trees,
infected with colour as the light died back,
we've settled to greyness: fields behind gauze,

hedges feint in tracing-paper mists,
the sun diminished to a midday moon
and daylight degraded to the monochrome

of puritan weather. This healing cold
holds us to pared-down simplicities.
Now is the worst-case solstice time,

acutest angle of the shortest day,
a time to condemn the frippery of leaves
and know that trees stand deltas to the sky

producing nothing. A time to take your ease
in not knowing, in blankness, in vacuity.
This is the season that has married me.

II *Annunciation*

When first he painted the Virgin the friar filled
the space around her with angels' wings,
scalloped and plated, with skies of gold,

heavy with matter. He thought that he knew
that heaven was everywhere. He grew
older, wiser and found that he drew

more homely rooms with pots and beds,
but lavished his art on soft furnishings
and the turn of the waiting angel's wings

(still gorgeous with colour and precious dust).
Much later, he sensed that his God had withdrawn,
was spacious. On smaller frescoes he painted less,

let wall be wall, but drew in each lawn
the finer detail of sorrel and weeds.
Still later, he found his devotion drawn

to nothing – shadows hinted at hidden rooms,
at improbable arches, while the angel's news
shattered the Virgin, who became a view

as open as virtue, her collapsing planes
easy and vacant as the evening breeze
that had brought a plain angel to his grateful knees.

III

I've made friends with nothing and have found
it is a husband. See these wedding rings?
Two eyes through which I see everything

but not as I used to. Importance leaves me cold,
as does all information that is classed as 'news'.
I like those events that the centre ignores:

small branches falling, the slow decay
of wood into humus, how a puddle's eye
silts up slowly, till, eventually,

the birds can't bathe there. I admire the edge;
the sides of roads where the ragwort blooms
low but exotic in the traffic fumes;

the scruffy ponies in a scrubland field
like bits of a jigsaw you can't complete;
the colour of rubbish in a stagnant leat.

These are rarest enjoyments, for connoisseurs
of blankness, an acquired taste,
once recognised, it's impossible to shake,

this thirst for the lovely commonplace.
It's offered me freedom, so I choose to stay.
And I thought my heart had been given away.

IV

He started to transform himself in sixty-three,
though few of us knew it at the very start
or suspected his goal was transparency.

We only noticed that he'd disappear
from time to time off the factory floor.
We covered, but his absences grew longer

till, for all our lying, he was finally caught
by the foreman in the locker room,
tied up in a clear chrysalis of thought.

Nothing would shift him, so he got the sack,
but took it quite calmly. When I walked him home
he explained that there was no turning back

from his self-translation. The scales of a butterfly
are not coloured at all, but are shingles of white
which simply accept the prismatics of light

in spectacular patterns. That humility
was what he was after. I met him often
and watched his skin's translucency

deepen with practice, so that his derm
and epidermis were transmogrified.
He was able to earn some cash on the side

as a medical specimen while muscles and veins
were still visible and then even more
for the major organs as he became pure

through his praying (this after his wife
had sued him for lack of comfort and joy
in their marriage) but by now his life

was simply reflective. I could only discern
his shape in the sunshine, so purged was he
of his heaviness and opacity.

He knew he was nothing. Through him I saw
colours shades deeper than ever before
and detail: the ratchets on a snail's rough tongue,

the way light bruises, how people fall
to weakness through beauty and when we came
to him for vision, he accepted us all,

made us more real, gave us ourselves
redeemed in the justice of his paraphrase,
the vivid compassion of his body's gaze.

V *'A Calm'*

'Nothing is happening everywhere,
if only we knew it. Take these clouds,
our most expensive purchase to date,

five million for a fleet becalmed
off the coast of nowhere. I like the restraint
that chose this lack of action in paint,

this moment of poise between travel and rain –
cumulonimbus in a threatening sky,
horizon, cumulonimbus again

as water gives the air its rhyme
and the pressure keeps dropping. An oily tide
buoys up a barrel by the coaster's side,

emptied, no doubt, by the sailors on board
waiting, tipsy, for their lives to begin
again with the weather. The clouds close in

but this boredom's far richer than anything
that can happen inside it – than the wind, than a port,
or the storm that will wipe out this moment of nought.'

'A Calm': a painting by Jan van de Capelle,
newly acquired by the National Museum of Wales.

VI

The monk says nothing, finger to his lips
and day begins inside his silences.
First dawn then birdsong fill the gaps

his love has left them. He's withdrawn
to let things happen. His humility
has allowed two kinds of ordinary –

sparrows and starlings – to fight it out
over the fruit of a backyard tree
and against the blackbirds. His nonentity

is a fertile garden, fed by the well
of a perfect cipher, and the water's cool,
most nourishing. He drinks his fill

and cities happen in his fissured mind,
motorways, roadblocks. He is host
to ecosystems that sustain us all,

for our lives depend on his emptiness.
His attention flickers. He turns away
to something and destroys our day.

Squaring the Circle

Mary of Burgundy (1457-1482)

Philip the Handsome (1478-1505) = *Joanna the Mad* (1479-1555)

Here is the body
of Mary of Burgundy
with a box containing the heart
of her son,
Philip the Handsome.
Was it wise
to become
so centralised?

In a convent in Spain
Joanna the Mad,
enflamed by all
the women he had,
keeps guard at his body
inflamed by the heat
of the gothic fever
that's to be her fate –
her Castilian hate.

For who's to say
where his real heart lay?

And in the Salle des Mariages
the members of Mary's entourage
have been hung like portraits,
so they never think
of rearranging this odd ménage
of three dominions
all out of sync.

For these
are not bodies
but polities
and the truth is
that having Philip back
has given his mother
a heart attack.

The Soul Mine

The guidebook directed us to a nunnery
where no one spoke English.
Nearby, a quarry
was blasting for granite,
working to free
buildings and walls from the rockery
of rubble. In a dark chapel
a nun, almost silent, mined the air
making a statue of breathing and prayer.

Heroic sisters! They are the quarry
of a spirit that hunts them.
Love is predatory,
best met with stillness
and passivity.
The smashed heart is its own safety.
Water flows, soft, from the rock.
Minds and minerals submit to their loads:
cold stones that women kiss explode.

A Fanciful Marriage

So it came that Too Little married Too Much
and all pronounced it an ideal match,
as tending towards the golden mean:

a chance for Too Much to be somewhat less,
for Too Little to wax into something more.
The priest and the guests felt sure it was blessed.

'O cup to my water, O my weather vane!'
'Rain to my drought, my gentle hurricane!'
They looked lovely in matching metonymies.

But they left out one guest – the Literal –
who sneaked, unseen, into the hall
to utter her matter-of-fact revenge:

'See things as they are, for only a fool
can pretend a cracked cup can ever be full
or that mankind can catch it when brightness falls.'

For a while they were fine. Too Little grew fat
and, filling out to his marriage vows,
abandoned his famine in favour of feast.

But his viscera got him. No conjugal bliss
could stop him from turning away in disgust.
Soon he had slid into someone less,

past least, until he was merely some,
an honest-to-goodness matchstick man –
he'd tried to be golden, but had ended up mean.

Too Much grew rampant at his mutiny
and ditched her honeymoon regime
to rail against the insults of time.

Dressed in gowns of bitter glory,
she flung floods at her husband's thing of stone,
wove storms of illusion, but woke alone

to worry the winds to their proper paths,
and hold up huge cities by force of will,
keeping coal to its seams beneath the hills.

But all was not lost for, during a lull,
he lifted his siege, she breached his wall
and they had a bit of the actual.

Surprise! A daughter! and on her face
the seven letters of 'Homo Dei'
spelt promise, reliance and simple grace

(if only they'd seen it). So, day by day,
their hopes grew high on her infant health,
bridge of their bloods, their commonwealth,

the map that would chart their antipodes!
The Literal sighed and the child fell asleep
between her parents' parentheses.

She grew and they redrew their battle lines
to criss-cross their daughter, who lived in fear
that she'd always fall short of their metaphors.

A blank, she became the board for their games:
The words on her face were never the same
as they played hard scrabble with desperate hands...

compliance, no, defiance. These shifting sands
blunted her features, dulled her hair
as she mimicked cold triumph or old despair,

sure that her mirror could save their souls.
Till her own went missing. Then, how she ran,
chasing its radiant flickering

down alleys of phantasmagoria
that ravish travellers from what they are,
dim waters that make the near far

and all holding impossible, where the past
takes hostages to make itself last.
Still her satellite danced ahead,

glinting through chasms, past chimeras
that flayed her of feeling and left her for dead.
Her parents grew anxious and, quiet with dread,

went looking for her, hand in hand.
Together they tried to understand
how their marriage had slid so wide of the mark.

Too Little wept and Too Much let him be....
They finally found her where a troupe of tropes
had turned her to pure geometry.

High in electric air she hung
too like a triangle to hear
how they wanted her down from the sizzling wire;

and around the echoing chamber
resplendent reflections glided and glanced
away from the empty darkness of her.

They stood transfixed, their faces two noughts.
'Come down!' called Too Little, but his daughter's pain
wound her up tighter and started a spin.

But somehow she'd glimpsed their frightened eyes,
a spirit level to her tilting skies.
She stirred but, held back by stunning bolts,

described another sickening arc
for she had remembered, and brittle tears
fell in a brilliant shower of sparks.

'Help her', they prayed to the Literal,
'save her from this human fall,
for we can do nothing for her as we are.'

At that the uninvited guest
stepped from the shadows and gently unbound
the girl from her cradle and bore her down

softly and, as the floor drew near,
she whispered: 'There's nothing further to fear
for I am your gravity and your grace,

the only contentment you'll ever know.
So remember this twisted parable of you.
Our lives begin as you touch the ground.'

And she set her down and, patient and mild,
showed them each other, then took them home –
a father, a mother, and a shaking child.

Welsh Espionage

I

'I dreamt they took me in for questioning
last night. They asked repeatedly about you:
Who were your friends? What exactly did they do?
I had my suspicions, but I didn't sing.

They seemed to think you were some kind of spy.
I stuck to my story. Did I know you well?
Did I have any secrets I would care to sell?
No. Nothing on you. I didn't have to lie.

But I got to thinking. Those weekends away,
those trips to Wales every now and then
to see the family, your mysterious men....
Tell me now, darling, whom did you betray?'

II

The Secret Service takes all kinds.
We keep them forever on our books,
men possessed of jigsaw minds
and boring, unobtrusive looks.
We like them with chameleon looks.

The agents on our danger list
are those possessed of total recall.
Sooner or later they can't resist
the terrible urge to tell it all.
Yes, the treason of telling it all.

This spying trip so far a great success.
Place smaller than I remembered, but less safe.
Softness of water harder to assess.

Close shave at the station when I asked my way.
Ticket collector quizzed me: Did I know
the pubs or the chapels better? Got away

with mumbling 'Neither' and then leaving fast.
I mustn't let on that I speak Welsh
or they're sure to connect me with my past

and that would be fatal to my enterprise.
Have checked all exits at the B & B
lest they should take me by surprise.

Trumpet player in room overhead
struck up in scales as I went out.
'The angels are coming,' someone said.

Suspicious couple from last night are gone.
Who are the Angels? Please run a check.
Landlord knows more than he's letting on.

I know too little and still feel too much
to be able to make a full report.
Project needs more research. Will keep in touch.

IV

A passing goods train makes the chapel quake
as the audience rises to sing its praise.
The fox-fur in front gives a sickening shake,
fixes the child with its terrible gaze.

Long pipes like icicles hang overhead
though the preacher's sweating with Sunday heat.
She hides by her father and hangs her head,
ashamed of sitting in the sinners' seat.

And while they're praying she opens her eyes,
looks daggers at a deacon's florid nape,
noting the details with retentive hate.
She thrills to think of all the outraged cries
when she's denounced them. There'll be no escape
from what she remembers. And she can wait.

V

Welsh was the mother tongue, English was his.
He taught her the body by fetishist quiz,
father and daughter on the bottom stair:
'Dy benelin yw *elbow*, dy wallt di yw *hair*,

chin yw dy ên di, *head* yw dy ben.'
She promptly forgot, made him do it again.
Then he folded her *dwrn* and, calling it fist,
held it to show her knuckles and wrist.

'Let's keep it from Mam, as a special surprise.
Lips are *gwefusau*, *llygaid* are eyes.'
Each part he touched in their secret game
thrilled as she whispered its English name.

The mother was livid when she was told.
'We agreed, no English till four years old!'
She listened upstairs, her head in a whirl.
Was it such a bad thing to be Daddy's girl?

VI

First love's eyes are open wide;
it thinks the world is on its side.
Youthful passion can't resist
the glamour of the terrorist.

Second love is at a loss,
victim of the double-cross.
Soon it's using little lies
to free itself. We're getting wise.

Third time round has learned to wait –
slow to love and slow to hate.
It cultivates the private eye,
the patience of the perfect spy.

VII *The Spy Comes Home*

Leave, if you like, but those you've left won't wait
to bear you witness once you've broken free.
Now pay the price of coming home too late.

Warmth I expected, or a loving hate,
the deserter resented for his liberty.
Leave, if you like, but those you've left won't wait.

Peer through the window at the leaded grate,
tap on the pane with the rain-soaked tree.
Now pay the price of coming home too late.

Steal away and time will confiscate
the place you hoarded in your memory.
Leave, if you like, but those you've left won't wait.

Who's to redeem the jaded reprobate,
if not the incurious in the family?
Now pay the price of coming home too late.

A row of graves by the chapel gate,
mouths as cold as their charity.
Leave, if you like, but those you've left won't wait.
Now pay the price of coming home too late.

VIII

Dressed in a sheath of black silk acetate
she arches her back. White fingers feel
her legs to check the seams are straight
and dead in line with each stiletto heel.

She knows she's dangerously svelte:
the darts are placed with consummate skill
to stress the cinching leather belt,
the batwing sleeves. She's dressed to kill.

Give her a chance and she'll love you to death –
she always gets her way with men.
But first she must suffer. 'Take a deep breath,
and we'll try to close that zip again.'

IX *Advice on Adultery*

The first rule is to pacify the wives
if you're presented as the golden hope
at the office party. You're pure of heart,
but know the value of your youthful looks.
Someone comments on your lovely back.
Talk to the women, and avoid the men.

In work they treat you like one of the men
and soon you're bored with the talk of the wives
who confide in you about this husband's back,
or that husband's ulcer. They sincerely hope
you'll never have children ... it ruins your looks.
And did you know David has a dicky heart?

You go to parties with a beating heart,
start an affair with one of the men.
The fact you've been taking care of your looks
doesn't escape the observant wives
who stare at you sourly. Cross your fingers and hope
that no one's been talking behind your back.

A trip to the Ladies. On your way back
one of them stops you for a heart to heart.
She hesitates, then expresses the hope
that you won't take offence, but men will be men,
and a young girl like you, with such striking looks....
She's heard nasty rumours from some of the wives.

She knows you're innocent, but the wives,
well, jump to conclusions from the way it looks....
In a rage, you resolve she won't get him back,
despite the pressure from the other wives.
They don't understand... you'll stick with the men,
only they are *au fait* with affairs of the heart.

You put it to him that you're living in hope.
He grants that you're beautiful, but looks
aren't everything. He's told the men,
who smirk and wink. So now you're back
to square one, but with a broken heart.
You make your peace with the patient wives.

Don't give up hope at the knowing looks.
Get your own back, have a change of heart:
Ignore the men, start sleeping with the wives.

X

From Craig y Foelallt I can see it all –
the church, the chapel, the dry-stone bridge,
the road that leads to the vicarage,
Catherine's house by the Village Hall.

They're playing football. From the hoots and cries
I count up the score: Llanddewi two,
the Visitors nil. Children I knew
have grown into farmers I don't recognise.

I watch the living, while overhead
two kites are working the valley floor,
looking for movement. Me they ignore
because I'm spying on the dead.

XI

So this is the man you dreamt I had betrayed.
I couldn't have saved him if I'd stayed.

He's old as his language. On his bony knees
his hands are buckled like wind-blown trees

that were straight in his youth. His eyes are dim,
brimming with water. If you talk to him

he'll mention people whom you never knew,
all in their graves. He hasn't a clue

who you are, or what it is you want
on your duty visits to Talybont.

This is how languages die – the tongue
forgetting what it knew by heart, the young

not understanding what, by rights, they should.
And vital intelligence is gone for good.

The Bad Shepherd

Cornelius Varro knows his husbandry
and he maintains a flourishing estate:
'My mutes stand guard at the entrance gate.
Vowels I lodge with my hired men,
half-vowels sit by the cattle pen.
Of course, I let the spirants work the field,
as they're teaching the clover how to yield
to consonantal chimings from the church.'
But I'm uncouth and keep lip service back.

For I'm the one who herds his fields of wheat,
speaks softly till the stalks are white,
the ripe ears heavy. Then I sow my spite
and laugh to see how the rows stampede,
as I spread sedition with the highland wind
till they're wrecked and broken. Then he sends men round
and I watch in silence as they slowly reap
his yearly tribute from my grudging ground.

Going Primitive

Who can resist a didgeridoo
in the middle of Queen St – not one, but three
from the Northern Territory,
each one more deeply, eucalyptically rude?

For the builders have lost the passers-by
who are drawn like water to the swirl and squelch,
the monstrous plumbing of his breath,
sucked in and further, and then atomised,

breathed out in stiff shirts and office skirts
but feeling looser....
A wasp photographer
snaps the man from all angles for something sweet

and the women, who sweat at his embouchure,
grow broad as rivers to his narrow lips,
dirty as deltas, with silting hips
and alluvial bosoms. The men, unsure,

cower behind their totem wives,
puny and trouty; now chimpanzees
swing through the scaffolding with ease
and screech with the newly arrived macaws;

cranes buck and bow and the wooden thrum
makes men recall a biography
of sludge and savannah, how it was when the sky
arched its blue back and started to come.

The Reference Library
(to open the sixth-form library at Ysgol Gyfun Rhydfelen)

Elsewhere a leather-bound volume holds the sum
of what a distant century knew
of cosmology and Christendom,
of how to cook with feverfew;

how to make silk; how Latin spread
like roads across a kingdom which then fell
to rhetoric and laws and lead
but let prophetic fishes tell

their older stories, ones of mortal sin,
how men of rock were spawned from tors
with tongues of granite, breathing whin
which stopped the logical conquerors.

How comprehensive! Look around you now:
concordances are a thumbnail wide,
a wafer-thin thesaurus shows you how
new languages are regicides;

there are directories of heads of state,
files of disease with their listed cures,
transport technologies to contemplate,
anatomies of the urban poor...

But compared to you, an encyclopaedia
is thin provision. Throw the big tomes out,
and the almanacs with their logorrhoea.
Read first the lexicons of your own doubt,

for in your spines and not in those of books,
lies the way to live well, the best library;
for the erudition of your open looks
shall turn old words to new theologies.

Parables AND *Faxes*

Parables AND Faxes

I   FAX

The hum was there from before the start:
my mother, a baby, on her sister's lap
and the hive behind them, its whitewashed slats
squat as a stanza. I can feel its heat

and the sepia blur of a landing bee
dancing the scents of a stamen he came
to offer in steps to the greedy comb
and trade in the world for geometry.

We are all transformers: we change what we see
into sap and succour; the hive's a machine
that hoards up the substance for its working soul,
a Madonna of amber and electricity.

And now in my dreams the neutrinos sing
from the hive in the corner and the atom's halls
are held up by talking, by great upheavals
and voices so truthful that snatches heard fling

all sense into terror, the square room round,
the set world bucking. What is this grace
which keeps knowing so near us, but the lid in place,
that insists on the gift of a throbbing ground?

After a winter out in the cold
the tramp was honking.

They broke open the seals with trembling hands.

In death he looked almost beautiful
but was foul when he woke for his photograph
at the start of his treatment.

They were scared by the glint of guardian eyes
till they knew them for statues.

So bad was the smell that they cut off his clothes
and burned them, ceremoniously.

From that moment they knew that this prince was great...

Fungus grew out of the doctors' mouths
and the nurses breathed flowers...

...for his flesh was tectonic plates of gold
and under that, honey, black with the burn
of all those millennia...

...Heminevrin and Temazepam....

the omnipotent tibia shattered by air,
his fingers sticking to the scarab rings,
his pelvis plundered....

Much later, they danced in their dressing-gowns
under the moon of the white clock's face
(*and the horns of Isis*), no cords, and no belts,
profile Pharaonic, with a Nubian grace,
pouring libations from dementia's wine:
The resurrected, they have swallowed time.

We lived off the Street of Incendiaries
the winter the city finally fell
and yielded to the infidel.

Our Lord, the Elephant of God,
was captured and tortured by slow degrees
as the city lost its integrity.

The arrows of the mercenaries
rained on us like germs, till the crumbling walls
succumbed at last to the siege's disease.

But I remember our immunity:
the starlings' static in sighing trees,
the flames of caged canaries,

green courtyards, bromeliads licking the light
from under the tamarinds; and Mary's crown
like snakes, her wrath our fortune,

and the cool burn of her composure
the dark centre of our best desires,
our safety lodged in her danger.

Forgive us. For now, this St Lucy's Day
the ruined city is offered in praise
back to the sun and the strengthening sky

and the broken begin to prophesy
through solstice and slaughter to a citadel
that none but the routed shall occupy.

It's impossible, but it's happening:

Your face, a river, runs from yesterday;
your words, a fountain, fall back into sleep

to rise and break out in deliberate rain.
You are poise and pivot and swing the moon

on its cantilever till the known skies tilt
into reflection. You are blindness felt,

the gravity pull of an absent light;
you're the seed inside the sacrament.

You are all that's easy, all that flies in the face
of the will that prefers its flowers forced

while I...I am the unravelling twine
whose brokenness is laid in time

to give purchase to crystals till my spacious halls
shall house you and the raven's call,

so still in the grove you could drink your fill
of blackness from its brimming well.

Saxons are vertical,
circles we,
hence the mutual hostility.
They climb, we spiral;
who shall be
the better in their eternity?

Curls tend to churls
while ladders rise;
they are legs and we the eyes
that watch the progress of the earls
across the skies
over the clods they patronise.

We are return
but progress they,
roundabout versus motorway.
We borrow but they always own
the deeds of day,
certificates for right of way.

A thane is bright,
no plodder he,
an apex of geometry
that draws the Angles to their heights;
though fantasy
must know the fear of gravity.

The humble are fly
and know the crown
for an O in which a man can drown
or drink his death – such irony
is for the prone
who praise the good they'll never own.

She wants to be transported all the time
but has fallen further than the theatre floor,
the girl whose pain moves like a *pas-de-deux*,
the sordid partnering the sublime.

The world falls upwards – beat it down
with booze and *bourrées*, *entrechats* and speed;
for the perfect *jeté* and the sharp aside
disguise the danger of the looming ground

once you have climbed your staircases of air
and blown your back-ups and you see, below,
how car tops look like plumped-up pillows
and – here it comes – concrete like an easy chair.

So the Lord said: 'Eat this scroll.'
I did and it was sweet and light and warm
and filled my belly. But I didn't speak
for all His urgings. Tolstoy's good
and Kafka nourishing. I lick

the fat from all the books I can
in the shops at lunchtime – Ovid, Byron, Keats....
The assistants know me, but they let me feast
on spaghetti sentences if I don't break the spines
of paperbacks and I replace them fast

so buyers never know their books
are licked of God. I am voracious
for the Word – a lexicon is wine
to me and wafer, so that home, at night,
I ruminate on all that's mine

inside these messages. I am the fruit
of God's expressiveness to man.
I grow on libraries, suck the grapes
of Os and uncials and still –
no prophecies. When I am ripe

I shall know and then you'll see the caravans,
processions, fleets, parades come from my mouth
as I spew up cities, colonies of words
and flocks of sentences with full-stop birds
and then, when I'm empty I shall open wide

and out will come fountains for the chosen few
to bathe in as time falls into brilliant pools,
translucent and ruined. Meantime I shall grow
stony with knowing, and my granite tongue
shall thirst (God's gargoyle!) for these blessings' blows.

(*WESTERN MAIL* HEADLINE, MARCH 1928)

The dog did it and that's definite.
Luther was sound before he was bit
and we still don't believe the magistrate

who found the damned mongrel innocent
of Uncle Luther's mania.
There must have been hydrophobia

(though the records don't show it and the dog was put down).
He was mad when we called the policeman in,
breaking the furniture and raving

with chthonic fury about a Cerberus
who bit him as he tried to pass
through underworld caves to get back to us,

for he was the Rhondda's Persephone.
The dog bite, he howled, would guarantee
his return to inferno, his immortality.

In the end, both uncle and mongrel died.
But we always remembered what Luther had said
about havoc and Hades. Now we cross the road

to avoid all guard dogs – a family fear.
For if it wasn't the dog, then it was Luther
and sour-breathed Cerberus is always too near.

King William conquered the British Isles
by griffin and dragons with knots in their tails:
God's order in the borders of time –
centaurs rampant and leopards tame
with the lambs they slaughtered and the crane
kind to the wolf that killed it. Now a wife
opens her arms in a garden, starts a gale
that impregnates the Normans' sails
and brings them in force to Pevensey.
Now the peacock and the harpie cry
out so Saxons die and horses fall
while, in the border, ornament is all
and trees that are rooted in history
hold birds more real than the sights they see
until the wyverns are put to rout
by human bodies that blot the border out.

X   FAX

Today set sail like a cruising ship
taking us with it, so we waved goodbye
to the selves that we were yesterday
and left them ashore like a memory
while we launched out on the open sea,
were travelling! The breeze grew stiff
so we grabbed the railings, tasted the surf
as the sky came towards us, the equator noon
a place to pass us, while the tropics of tea
swung over us and straight on by
as time kept sailing and we hung on,
admiring the vistas of being away
while the shadows died down from the flames of day
and we coasted around a long headland of sky
and into night's port while, out in the bay
tomorrow called out like a ringing buoy.

It seemed a simple case of opulence,
when diggers discovered the marble pool
still edged in lapis lazuli and gold
with dolphin mosaics under a portico,
all placed so the swimmer could seem to dive
into the wealth of the valley below.

But mercy's a mystery, and takes time to see.
Another pool outside the palace gates,
its bottom cluttered with unclaimed lamps
knocked over by lepers as they shuffled, late,
to bathe there in secret, never thinking that now
we see them immersing themselves in pure light.

My God! in the hands of a lunatic
and taken hostage!
One mistake
and he and I could both be dead,
like flies on a windowsill.
He's out of his head

on greed and wanting and he'll do me in
if he's not seen to.
I can never win
this game of blind because I'm the buff.
I supply his demands
but it's never enough

to appease him. He can live for days
on nothing but will
until he's crazed
on making things happen and on holding fire.
They say I love him
but it's only fear

of life without him, all on my own,
without the excitement
or the charm of a gun
to my head, feeling wanted, part of a 'we',
not perched on a lonely
column of I.

And yet, if I choose, he will fall away,
for a soul is far stronger
than the rampant me
with its threats and its deadlines. Pity his end,
a defeat he will never
understand

while I, undiminished, will carry on,
a nothing, transparent,
not on the run
but moving much faster and able to feel
the speed of travelling
while perfectly still.

Something shifted and the landscape breathed,
killing two thousand – the Angel of the Lord
was with us, bless this deadly Lord

and his fatal Angel who has left, freeze-framed,
these lives in emblem: father holding son,
a mother running. Angel of the Lord,

who stopped the messenger on the dusty road
and spread out his body, a forgotten word
in a dying language. Angel of the Lord

who undressed the elders as they tried to flee
then took them from their histories,
Angel who teaches that we do not see

but are seen by greatness, held then killed
by the swiftest glance, that those who win
are those who lose the fight with him,

the wrestling Angel, who takes everything,
as is his right: the Angel of the Lord,
wielding the evening breeze as his sword.

This Mahādeva is a great white dog
who sets out with me on a winter walk
in snowy mountains, though he never stays.
He is also the god who suddenly appears
to herd men's souls, a palindrome, a way

of walking, though the world withdraws
from us in mist, as faith draws back from words,
to leave us groping. Hear him pant behind,
circling my path then passing, pulled ahead
by smells that say this is his land

though I keep to the path, as farmers shoot for rain
and other creatures. In the fields around
the melt is making continents of snow
and slopes are shading into mackerel skies
that hide him from me. Now as I go

rain brings down mist and I find that I wear
thousands of diamonds on clothes and hair
and now it is white-out and behind I hear
that Mahādeva the wolf is here,
hungry for wonder, thirsting for fear.

Mahādeva, the 'god who suddenly appears' is a form of
the Hindu god Siva. A friend's dog is named after him.

Talking of eating, did you see those crows
on the Peñas Grajeras as they gathered at dusk
in their hundreds, till the cliffs were dark

with rifts and gossip? Rook-saturated rock
seethed with a sleekness that shone in the gloom
as if the birds were devouring time

and making the rapid twilight gleam
with calls that drew the moon's wafer near.
This ancient pact was enacted there:

man's failure feeds the ravens' hunger
and they, in time, remind the man
that the filth of his own carrion –

humiliation, lies and pain –
is transformed into manna; then, the watcher, in turn,
sees how the birds of blackness burn

his world to nothing and so he discerns
that shining ruin is his only creed,
that noxious night is most necessary bread.

Cliff of Rooks: behind the burial place
of St John of the Cross, Segovia.

She came to me
in a dream of enormous bosoms,
magnificent lallers,
not hers but mine,
that had grown from nothing,
ripened and swelled
till they overflowed my office blouse
and were...a phenomenon.
My colleagues looked on
but no one was rude
about my stupendous amplitude.

Word spread and other workers came
to see for themselves
so I fed them,
telling them all the while
of how it is that all is well
and how endlessly
the miracle welled up in me
of her kindness and generosity.

And then the hall
was filled with my hair
and knowing this
was really her
we swam in the whorls
of her fragrant care

and nobody minded
that no work was done
for Tara held us
in her plenitude,
for her help is warm,
her breath is food!

Tara is a Buddhist deity, especially
helpful in overcoming difficulties.

It's seldom we know how lucky we are.
A dragon's head smokes in the darkening air
and talk turns to wonder – how the stars are near,
how life burns the bones of those who are far
in time to embers more fragrant and charred
than the bonfire before us.

                              The dragon roars on,
blotting out sour cherry and lime,
for his sentences blind us – he talks of Beauty
that bound him tight with her terrible calm
and brought him, grotesque, to his grateful knees,
a monster for ever. We feel her take aim
from the shadows and shush as we see the trees
draw near with our dying days in their arms.

   (1916)

And now I remember the tall hussar
who gave me the halo of telegraph wire
which I wound round my body at the age of six.
Since then my hearing's been strangely acute,
for I watched as the workmen erected a line
of identical crosses all the way down
to the river that kept on discussing itself
out through the village, on to somewhere's sea....
He was huge in his dolman and when he saw

my delight at the splitting and hewing of wood
he called me closer to his brilliant braid
then the world dipped and I could see the way
that men were cradled in the criss-cross tree,
hammering nonsense, till they left one man
like a Christ on the wire there, hanging alone
but listening to something that no one else heard.
My heart beat in dashes back down on the ground
and I knew that I'd learn how to understand

the metal's despatches. Now, since the war
I've crossed high passes to talk in Morse
to other transmitters, leading horses piled high
with the weight of talking, till I found my way
here to the trenches, to the news of troops,
disasters and weather, where now I'm stretched out,
nerves copper and all my circuits aware
they're transmitting a man on a wheel of barbed wire,
nothing but message, still tapping out fire.

For the one
who said yes,
how many
said no?

Of course,
there was
the Sumatran who refused
and then the Nubian,
then the Swede,
who shied away
from bearing the Word,
though the chance
was offered...
a Finn, a Chinese....
Declining politely
they carried on
with the dusting
or with its equivalent
so the question
was left

to an Indian, a Lapp,
petitioned by God
for outrageous assent,
for in sweetest closeness
all being is rent.

But those who said no
for ever knew
they were damned
to the daily
as they'd disallowed
reality's madness,
its astonishment.

So the moment passed
and the fissure closed,
an angel withdrew,
no message sent,
and the lady prepared
her adequate meal
– food of free will –
from which God
a while longer
was absent.

XX *Resurgence Pool*   FAX

This is the place where the boys get killed –
not underground, where the river flows
in lakes so reflective nobody knows
where dark ends and where new currents begin.
No, this is the danger – where the water flings

itself to the light, so cold it can tear
all breath from a body, as it speaks its words
of strength and revival and opens wide,
looking like reason, persuading the young
whom it drowns in the lies of its treacherous tongue

And this, too, is love:

The tanker *Cliona* on the Coral Sea,
called in to assist a hospital ship
hit by the Japs and sinking in flames.
The tanker, which carries a cargo of fuel
so flammable hammers are banned on deck,
for fear their sparks might ignite stray gas,
draws near to the liner. Nurses drop down
and patients are winched from the burning hulk
to the *Cliona*, which is carrying death
but Captain O'Hara holds the ship near
to its ultimate danger and the searing heat
blisters their faces – love's garment is pain
and impossible daring. Now the undertow
brings them still closer, the whole crew burns
in anticipation of the moment she blows
and still she doesn't – how long can she last
before physical logic remembers the load –
each moment's precious, lent from the blast –
before love and its opposite crash and explode?

So the world offers itself in love:
A park on a Sunday with a simple band,
oom-pah-pah under the cherry tree.
What could be more ordinary?

But time divided the music like this:
To open, an easy ball was thrown,
caught with a lunge of the skirt, a laugh,
two children (related) running around
pursued by a dog who can't get enough
municipal smells from the mellow sound
which starts to repeat – the ball gets thrown,
till, this time, the girl runs round on her own,
followed by dog with a lolloping tongue.

Then the reprise: ball in an arc,
not fumbled now but moving free
from one hand to another, the dog, then three
youngsters (must be one family)
chased by the music; the sun goes in,
world goes flat, dog takes a break,
but the children are back, each one a repeat
with variations and, in their wake,
a blackbird bouncing as crescendo and ball
arch over the moment and let them all through,
toddler chasing the other two,
dog yapping, happy having caught a ball
in the doily shade of the cherry tree
where the baton beat out eternity
for a moment before we went home for our tea.

Not all statues can change allegiances.
These are recusants that have been seized
and brought to this park by the new régime
to be hung by crane for political crimes

and out-of-date gestures. An historical wind
blows iron trousers against communist limbs
from different directions, as men in suits
(there are three Lenins at the entrance gate)

regard naked heroes, all muscle and thrust,
who were happy to bare their collective chests
to lead the people. Now they direct
the starling traffic and orchard troops

into the thick of the afternoon
in which nothing happens, where they gesture alone.
Before they were orators – men were their words
and iron foundries their strongest verbs

but now they avoid each other's eyes
but hear as the workmen take their ease,
smoking behind them, and they're forced to see
a concrete-mixer decide their history.

I saw a vision:
In a place called Pripyat
something exploded
from inside a tomb.
In the next room
someone was washing
as the geigers roared
and despite their scourging
the showers' rods
failed to restore
innocence
to the reactor's core.

The fire spread
and the roof tops burned
to show where a bride
and her nuclear groom
turned water to wormwood
while men in lead
joined in the dancing,
already dead.

And there, beyond the reactor's walls,
where Judas has hung himself,
Christ explodes
pointing a finger
as the isotopes
massacre children
on the vision's slopes.

And further out
Elijah's birds
feed him with darkness
by the motorway
and men are turned black
by the light of day.

And then, even further,
at the edge of time
Christ is baptised
in a gentle stream
and fish come to nibble,
the stars to see
God become one
with the burning flesh
that falls from men's bones
at the blinding flash

of his slightest appearance,
so the saints come to watch,
their haloes like moons,
burning like sixty thousand moons.

XXV   *Parables and Faxes*

A saint from the east
and a saint from the west
decided to travel so that they met.
The day they appointed the sun was hot
so the saint from the east was burnt on his neck,
the one from the west had a flaming face
when they settled on opposite banks of a stream
for holy conversation.

West was Parable, dazzled by the sun,
crows' feet showing how he used his eyes
to squint and focus, distance and transform
hints from nature into another order
which his imagination could explain.

East was Fax, straight observation,
simple facts lit from afar,
seen in themselves by long attention
and strict devotion to things as they are –
not Parable's similes, but metaphor.

Said Fax to Parable: 'How can you guess
what all you see can begin to mean?'
And Parable back: 'How can *you* bless
the chaotic surface that resists the sign?'

They argued until the sun wheeled round,
throwing two shadow saints on the ground.
Slowly they both began to cool
and language was left on their beards like rime,
their words in scrolls, which dropped from their hands,
as they stood, still struggling to understand
how they could shake off tyrant time
and still the stream laughed past in a line,
praying its way to the lexicon sea,
to nonsense and nonentity.

And then they knew they were bound to fail
and once they knew this they were suddenly full
of a better emptiness, wordless and wide,
which was known and tasted and felt like a flood
of breath in which all sense must lie,

brilliant like bubbles, to be quickly burst.
And they knew this was right by the quenching thirst
which turned them – one with his face to the sun,
the other his neck – and sent them home
to do what they could with provisional praise
and their partial vision, both overcome
by a conversation they'd scarcely begun.

ZERO GRAVITY

(1998)

I

Zero Gravity

ZERO GRAVITY

A Space Requiem

In memory of my sister-in-law
Jacqueline Badham
(1944-1997)

and to commemorate the voyage of my cousin
Joe Tanner and the crew of Space Shuttle STS-82
to repair the Hubble Space Telescope
(February 1997)

'*The easiest way to think of the universe is as a sphere*
which is constantly expanding so that everything is
getting farther away from everything else.'

SPACE FACTS

I PROLOGUE

We watched you go
in glory: Shuttle,
comet, sister-in-law.

The one came back.
The other two
went further. Love's an attack

on time. The whole damn thing
explodes, leaving
us with our count-down days

still more than zero.
My theme is change.
My point of view

ecstatic. See how speed
transforms us? Didn't you know
that time's a fiction? We don't need

it for travel. Distance
is a matter of seeing;
faith, a science

of feeling faint objects.
Of course, this is no
consolation as we watch you go

on your dangerous journeys.
This out of mind
hurts badly when you're left behind.

Don't leave us.
We have more to say
before the darkness. Don't go. Stay

a little longer. But you're out of reach
already. Above us the sky
sees with its trillion trillion eyes.

II

Day one at the Wakulla Beach Motel.
There are sixty of us here for the launch.
The kids have found lizards down by the pool,
been shopping in Ron Jon's. I mooch
and admire new body boards. My afternoon's
spent watching them surfing. The sea's my skirt,
breakers my petticoat. Along the seams
of rollers I watch cousins fall without getting hurt
as pelicans button the evening's blouse
into the rollers. The brothers wait,
each head a planet in the shallows' blaze.
They're blind to all others, are a constella-
tion whose gravity makes them surge forward, race
one another, arms flailing, for the broken spume
where they rise, bodies burnished, run back to the place
agreed on for jumping. They laugh in the foam
and I see eclipses, ellipses in the seethe
of a brash outer space. But here they can breathe.

III

It looks like she's drowning
in a linen tide.
They bring babies like cameras
to her bedside

because they can't see dying.
She looks too well
to be leaving. She listens
to anecdotes we tell –

how we met and got married.
She recounts a story:
her friend went stark mad
carrying, feeding, bleeding – all three

at once. She tried to bury
herself in Barry Island sand.
Her prayer plant has flowered
after seven years. She sends

Robert to fetch it from System St.
She thinks a bee sting
started the cancer.
We can't say a thing.

IV

Bored early morning down on Cocoa Beach,
the kids build castles. I know my history,
so after they've heaped up their Norman keep
(with flags of seaweed) I draw Caerphilly's
concentric fortress. Five-year-old Mary,
who's bringing us shells as they come to hand,
announces, surprised: 'I am the boss of me.'
She has a centre. In our busy sand
we throw up ramparts, a ring of walls
which Sarah crenellates. Being self-contained
can be very stylish – we plan boiling oil!
But soon we're in trouble with what we've designed.
So much for our plans to be fortified.
Our citadel falls to a routine tide.

V

First time I saw the comet, I finally knew
that I'd always love him. I watched it go,

dead starlight headed for a dying sun
then away into darkness. It was gone

before we knew what its brilliance meant,
a human moment in immense

spirals of nothing. I feel his pull
in my blood salts. The comet's tail

is a searchlight from another point,
and the point is once you've given your heart

there are no replacements. Oh, your soul,
if that can escape from its own black hole.

VI

Last suppers, I fancy, are always wide-screen.
I see this one in snapshot: your brothers are rhymes
with you and each other. John has a shiner
from surfing. Already we've started counting time
backwards to zero. The Shuttle processed
out like an idol to its pagan pad.
It stands by its scaffold, being tended and blessed
by priestly technicians. You refuse to feel sad,
can't wait for your coming wedding with speed
out into weightlessness. We watch you dress
in your orange space suit, a Hindu bride,
with wires like henna for your loveliness.
You carry your helmet like a severed head.
We think of you as already dead.

VII

Her voyage is inwards.
Now looking back
is a matter of passing events.
She makes for the dark

of not being human.
In turn she recalls
giving birth to Robert;
further back, a fall

while pregnant, the bathroom floor
of slate that saved her.
Silk parachute dresses
just after the war.

A bay tree, a garden, Victoria plums.
Then nothing before the age of ten
when a man attacked her.
It must be that pain

accelerates something.
Her speeding mind
leaves us in the present,
a long way behind.

VIII

Thousands arrive when a bird's about to fly,
crowding the causeways. 'Houston. Weather is a go
and counting.' I pray for you as you lie
on your back facing upwards. A placard shows
local, Shuttle and universal time.
Numbers run out. Zero always comes.
'Main engines are gimballed' and I'm
not ready for this, but clouds of steam
billow out sideways and a sudden spark
lifts the rocket on a collective roar
that comes from inside us. With a sonic crack
the spaceship explodes to a flower of fire
on the scaffold's stamen. We sob and swear,
helpless, but we're lifting a sun
with our love's attention, we hear
the Shuttle's death rattle as it overcomes
its own weight with glory, setting car alarms
off in the Keys and then it's gone
out of this time zone, into the calm
of black and we've lost the lemon dawn
your vanishing made. At the viewing site
we pick oranges for your missing light.

IX

The day before
she went she said
'Nothing matters.'
Now that she's dead

she's wiped herself off
our neural screens.
We no longer reach her.
But Jacqueline –

not her body,
nor her history,
nor our view of her –
now she's free

of her rubbish,
explodes on the eye
that perceives faint objects
on an inner sky.

She's our supernova,
sends joyous light
out of her ending.
To our delight

we fell neutrinos
from her ruined core,
can't take our eyes
off her stunning star.

X

Drew trips over his shadow by the pool
but picks himself up. We keep TVs on
like memorial flames, listen as Mission Control
gives cool instructions You are a sun
we follow, tracking your time over Africa,
a fauvist desert. We see you fall
past pointillist clouds in the Bahamas,
past glaciers, silent hurricanes, the Nile.
We're all provincials when it comes to maps
so we look out for Florida. The world's a road
above you – but you have no 'up',
only an orbit as you dive towards
an opal Pacific, now you see dawn
every ninety minutes. The Shuttle's a cliff
that's shearing, you on it, every way's 'down',
vertiginous plunging. It is yourself
you hold on to, till you lose your grip
on that, even. Then your soul's the ship.

XI

The second time the comet swung by
the knife went deeper. It hissed through the sky

like phosphorus on water. It marked a now,
an only-coming-once, a this-ness we knew

we'd keep forgetting. Its vapour trails
mimicked our voyage along ourselves,

our fire with each other, the endless cold
which surrounds that burning. Don't be fooled

by fireworks. It's no accident that *leave*
fails but still tries to rhyme with *love*.

XII

Only your eyesight can be used in space.
Now you've captured the telescope, nebulae
are birthmarks on your new-born face.
The sun's flare makes a Cyclops eye
on your visor. The new spectrograph
you've installed in the Hubble to replace the old
makes black holes leap closer, allows us to grasp
back in time through distance, to see stars unfold
in nuclear gardens, galaxies like sperm
swirled in water, rashes of young hot stars,
blood-clot catastrophes, febrile swarms
of stinging explosions. But what's far
doesn't stop hurting. Give me a gaze
that sees deep into systems through clouds of debris
to the heart's lone pulsar, let me be amazed
by the red shifts, the sheer luminosity
that plays all around us as we talk on the beach,
thinking there's nothing between us but speech.

XIII

What is her vanishing point?
Now that she's dead
but still close by
we assume she's heard

our conversations.
Out of sight? Out of mind?
On her inward journey
she's travelled beyond

the weight of remembering.
The g-force lifts
from her labouring chest.
Forgetting's a gift

of lightness. She's sped
vast distances
already, she's shed
her many bodies –

cancer, hope, regard,
marriage, forgiving.
Get rid of time
and everything's dancing,

forget straight lines,
all's blown away.
Now's honey from the bees of night,
music from the bees of day.

XIV

There are great advantages to having been dead.
They say that Lazarus never laughed again,
but I doubt it. Your space suit was a shroud
and at night you slept in a catacomb,
posed like a statue. So, having been
out to infinity, you experienced the heat
and roar of re-entry, blood in the veins
then, like a baby, had to find your feet
under you, stagger with weight, learn to cope
again with gravity. Next came the tour
of five states with a stopover in Europe.
You let people touch you, told what you saw.
This counts as a death and a second birth
within one lifetime. This point of view
is radical, its fruit must be mirth
at one's own unimportance and now, although
you're famous, a "someone", you might want much less.
Your laughter's a longing for weightlessness.

XV

Last sight of the comet. The sky's a screen
riddled with pinpricks, hung in between

me and what happened – a room not quite
hidden from me. Hale-Bopp's light

says something dazzling's taking place beyond,
involving moving. My mind

is silver nitrate, greedy for form
but I fail to grasp it here in this gloom.

Memory's a crude camera.
I wish you were seared on my retina

so I was blind to anything less
than your leaving. But the darkness

is kind. Dawn will heal with colour
my grief for your self-consuming core.

XVI EPILOGUE

A neighbourhood party
to welcome you home
from the Shuttle's tomb.

It's a wake in sunshine –
kids dive-bomb the pool.
My sense of scale's

exploded. Now I wear
glass beads like planets.
In my ears

are quasars. I have meteorites
for a bracelet, a constellation
necklace so bright

that, despite dark matter
in the heart,
I'm dazzled. 'Here' and 'there'

have flared together. A nonchalant father
throws Saturn rings.
Dive for them now and find everything.

II

Coconut Postcards

Coconut Postcards

A Goan Honeymoon

I

Wrapped in the palm trees' parentheses
the peninsula sighs. The repeated Vs
rustle of rain to come, but not tonight...
One tree is everything to us – is food, is light,
shelter and matting, drunkenness and shade,
boat or a ladder. We use it shamelessly –
eating it, plaiting it, as though it were made
solely for us, and still it gives more.
It's rooted in loving and has no fear
of its own exhaustion. Note how its star
is an asterisk: something important is planted here.

II

'You can have all the one-night stands you want
with me once we're married.' Along the waterfront
bee-eaters squeal as they strip the air
of its writing of insects; seagulls pilfer
wrist-watch crabs from the clock of the sea
which tells us our time. Like a silver boat
the moon has set sail on the light that we
must take as our monument today,
for we've married each other's dying. We pay
the ferryman's fare as he poles his way
past porpoise rip-tides in the darkening bay.

III

Back in his Sanskrit childhood, when a pile of stones
was a god, the Contractor was never alone,
was pantheistic. Now his head's a Kali
fixed to the sway of an avenger's body
in a ruined temple – a pose he holds for the wife.
He refuses to swim because of jellyfish,
which disgust him. He has lived a life
of thrust, of direction, he is a man of spine,
despising drift. But he fears the sting
of the floating organ, whose transparent design
can kill him by willing nothing.

IV

Entombed on their towels, the honeymooners gleam...
Alabaster limbs and gothic dreams
keep waiters away, for they lie in state.
Burnished by unguents they concentrate
on just being, now that all their delights
are formal, official. So their smiles are fixed –
eyes closed to the wheeling Brahminy kites
above, to the life around them, to the dissolute
hibiscus tongues, to the siren's alarms
as a baby's found buried in a palm tree's roots,
re-born from the earth into fostering arms.

V

Palm number eight is a toddy-tapping tree,
is fortunate, owns a family
which tends to its every need. In return
it allows them to place a strategic urn
over its sweetly bleeding stem
so that Polycarp d'Souza's still
is full. All night the palm tree bleeds for them.
At noon, girls gather in its fertile shade,
striped like tigers, for their husbandry's
ferocious – best marriage a tree could have made
against its main enemy, gravity.

VI

By the shack a man wants to clean out my ears
and then massage me. In the end I concur
and settle my lug-hole so that he can reach
its whorls. He digs and suddenly the beach
is louder. He picks out detritus, wax and more –
out comes a string of my memories –
leaving me light in the midday roar
of sand grains crashing and singing crabs. I'm
relieved of all the rubbish I've ever heard,
re-tuned, a transistor that can hear the first time
the call of the heart's hidden weaver-bird.

VII

On the beach you can practise our history
and crawl, amphibian, up from the sea
then under umbrellas to be something cool
in shorts and dark glasses. Look quizzical
as the sea's empty metre sighs at the feet
of a palm that carries flowers, acorns, fruit
all the same moment. At dusk we're freed
from shape into colour. On an opal tide
we swim: skin opens into lilacs and far
below the tuna's silver shoots through my side.
I reach out my tongue and lick Africa.

VIII

This place, like paradise, is better than us
but accepts us graciously, puts us at ease
with love's broad tolerance, so kind
that it only condemns the begrudging mind,
which exiles itself. For the moment, my dear,
simplification's the name of the game.
Set me up slowly like a folding chair
in the sun and, serenely, let's look out together
at the scenery and common life
which bless us repeatedly in the insect stir
of a palm-frond husband with his sea-breeze wife.

The Love of Furniture

I

I think today I'll wear my dresser,
the oak one with my grandmother's

china, the set her father bought for her
in Aberystwyth. I fancy lustrewear

and cake plates. Royal Albert's the future
of punk. Not everyone has hardwood to wear,

a set of brass-handled drawers.
But I have inheritance. So there.

II

I dreamt about us last night, my dear.
You were a wardrobe. Behind your doors

hung velvet dresses, satin shirts,
wet-look raincoats, watered-silk skirts

scented with lemon. You offered me more
than I'd ever dared to want before

and were capacious. So I picked out
a soft, well-tailored, shimmering suit

that sat just so then I made my way
out through the door and into the day.

III

The sofa bride is a pair of hips
for two to sit on. Upholstered lips

are plumped-up for love. She is a *chaise*
he yearns to be *longue* on. A promiscuous phase

has been polished over, a cabriole limb
that was gymnastic, restored to be prim,

fit for one owner. She'll take the strain
of his violence. Later he'll claim

that she tricked him, that they married too soon.
Settees with a past shouldn't wish for the moon.

IV

In battle all men shall remember
never to endanger the Admiral's furniture

on pain of death. It is essential
that the commander's gate-legged table

be stowed in the hold. It is worth far more
than the chap who made her. In times of war

chattels come first. If the hold is full
and the orlop deck cluttered with terrible

bodies then, seamen, be sure to launch a boat
and fill it with hautboy and with sideboard

for the enemy has agreed not to fire
on his fixtures and fittings. For, to be fair,

which of you can say that you've shown
such loyalty to a man of renown

or such service as his china and silver?
Lord Nelson's desk? Lord Nelson's easy chair?

V

There have been tales of great self-sacrifice
on the part of furniture. Take that chest of drawers

in the Kōbe earthquake. When the building fell
it flung itself down the tumbling stairwell

across its mistress who, pregnant, lay trapped
in the rubble for days. Its rosewood back

took the strain of girders. Its sturdiness
became her pelvis, allowed her to press

down on her daughter, helped her give birth
out of pulverised concrete and earth

by marquetry's artifice. Those dovetailed joints
gave life to another, though the effort meant

total collapse once the rescuers came
with shawls and shovels, ruined the frame

that had saved the baby. Now, once a year
on a certain date a woman and daughter

visit the grave on a building site
where fine wood was burnt. Lest they forget.

The Booming Bittern

Listen to that bittern boom.
You'll never see him. Tall reeds sway
and so does he,
courting invisibility.
Boom, bittern, boom.

See, he points up to the sky
in sympathy with wind-stirred sedge.
He has a body
but his camouflage
has made this bird all alibi.

This discretion's saved his life
so far. He sways in silence but he'll die
alone. The boom's
his only hope – his cry
might bring a brood of chicks, a wife.

To boom or not? A car alarm
risks nothing when it calls its mate.
But in a bog
you must be found, or not copulate.
So risk it, bittern. Boom, bittern, boom!

Good Dog!

All pets are part of one animal.
They look out at us from domestic eyes
hoping for food and a little love.
People who believe in reincarnation
feel the concern of departed relatives
shine from the heart of new-born pups,
so confide in them, spoil them.
A well-placed '*Om*' in a mongrel's ear
can save the soul of a dying dog.

Ours is theologian. He knows
that sticks in life are more reliable than cats
and that balls are better. Everything thrown
is instantly precious, well worth running for.
The river he loves and tends to wear
it often. A Baptist, he immerses himself
with total abandon so his otter soul
is renewed in the feeder with the bags of crisps
and ribbons of algae.
He wears the medal of himself with joy.

Something there is about a dog
draws conversation from frosty men
and available women. Trick for lonely boys and girls:
Get a dog. Walk him. For be it ugly or pure-bred,
a dog on a lead says: 'Here is a love
that makes its bargain with bad habits and smells,
the brute in a person, can accommodate needs
far other than its own, allows for beastliness.'

Some nights our lodger gets his favourite ball,
runs into the river and tramples the moon.

Peripheral Vision

I

Not everyone sees it, but I glimpsed the man
inside our terrier. We'd walked up the lane,
he stood back, a second, to let me in

through the gate, so courtly that, on my inner eye,
I saw him for the first time clearly
not a dog but a dish dressed in soft chamois,

tall like a prince, with thigh-length boots.
I said I would marry him. Sepia street lights
were our veil as, with love, I opened the locks

to our royal dwelling. Then, back on all fours,
he was wagging his tail by the kitchen door.
Beauty hides in the beast. This is the law.

II *The gods still walk around South Wales*

Caught in a traffic jam outside the Monico
cinema, a girl called idly on Apollo,
not meaning it. A stranger steps in. 'We'll go

up to the Beacons,' he said. 'I am
the answer to your prayers, a dangerous man,
not *deus ex machina* but lunatic in van.'

So she drove, directed by his Stanley knife,
fearing now for her hairdresser life
on B roads, till he'd ravished her enough

in lay-bys, near beauty-spot streams
to satisfy her kidnap dreams.
They say she made it all up. But how come

her joy, despite all the names she was called
by hacks and her neighbours? How come she recalled
such transport of love, a shower of gold?

III *View from an ocean-going liner*

Of course the poet Juan Ramón Jiménez
saw the sirens sink into mercury seas
off the coast of America. A disease

of the literal meant that his eyes
could focus on metaphor. Manatees
were mermaids. The Furies

came later. Once such figures are in the frame
you're finished. The way things seem is no longer home.
Sirens never stopped singing for him.

III

The Soul Candle

Soul Candles

I will
by the light
of my tinder soul
show you
the universe.

*

My hair's in streamers
of scorching air.
My mother stands over me
brushing my mane,
trying to tame it.
The plait explodes,
sloughs off to darkness
in roils of flame
fed on oils
of abandon.
My face is the same
under the roaring,
unravelling skeins.
I've plenty of tallow,
will burn a long time.

*

His revenge was ironic:
us two in the car
doused down with petrol,
one flick of a lighter
and everything's changed.
But his hate
brought us closer.
He gave us this,
deep in the sinews:
now that we share
the nerve ends' scorching,

our mutual heat
is a marriage,
this burning unbearable
but conjugal night.

*

His fierce bolt
keeps happening.
Even my veins
are made for his lightning.
I search for his volts
in stillness.
Soul's bright kite
tugs on its string,
nudging for danger,
for ruinous strike.

*

After the light show
which, from afar
was spectacular,
comes the real burning.
If you care
for me, make it go deep,
right down to the core,
past seeming, past knowing,
past being me,
where it smelts down all metals,
creating an ore
which is light crushed to weight.
Irradiate
my absence with the final spark
that is my extinction.
Now create
that half-life of speeding
through the seeing dark.

Flyover Elegies

(for Jane)

I

The traffic's been worse than ever this year,
straining bumper to choking tail,
inching towards the roundabout. We feel
that there's less oxygen to breathe in air,

less room for manoeuvre. Your flyover's arch
holds cars in a rainbow, its pot of gold
somewhere in town. Meanwhile, below,
mothers with pushchairs use the underpass,

struggle with shopping. These are the circles
of Dante's hell. There's the view
from the parapet, of course. But you,
like the transport, wanted somewhere else.

II

I remember the flyover being built.
The word was for freedom, for rising high
and swiftly, for avoiding a wait.
It was for cruising, for a wider view,
it was for people just passing through.

It sounded like death. All day the pile-
drivers thudded into the earth
with a sickening heartbeat. Flying takes viol-
ence and, the thing is, cement
needs a body before it's a monument.

III

At two in the morning the strongest hug
never touches the hurt. A mug

does something, but delivers less
than a bottle. Now your breath's

part-time, so it disappears,
comes back when you're desperate. Your tears

are diamond earrings. You crave
some rightness, but you don't believe

in anything less than pain: the tug
of concrete, with its credible hug.

IV

I think of you as I'm changing gear,
approaching the junction. In their cars

gilded commuters are longing for home,
profiles pharaonic on the sunset's tomb.

They play radio memories. Illness had made
you less than yourself. I ride

the flyover, clutching the wheel,
in awe of your uninhibited fall

into the streetlights' broken glass.
I envy the gesture but pity the glitz

that has tied up the traffic as your chiffon scarf,
made your belt a roundabout. I feel unsafe

at the apex, not because of despair.
My feet itch, like yours, for the giving air.

Drought

It needed torching, all that boring moor
above the village. I planted seeds
in several places till the spindly gorse

bore crimson flowers all around its own
of yellow, then collapsed in black.
Borders I planted with exotic blooms

then I watched as arson laid a smoky lawn
as far as the tree line. Beneath its grass
grew a snowdrop season of broken glass.

Talk with a Headache

I had this headache. Wherever I went
she followed, though I didn't want

her near me. As a hangover she'd lift
quite quickly. But a stab on the left

would start off a migraine, nausea, the lot
so that my darkened room was lit

by aura explosions. Her red-hot vice
was a cap of neuralgia and she wasn't averse

to a little tinnitus thrown in for fun.
I'd try a broadside of Nurofen

but nothing would shift her, not frozen peas,
nor wormwood. I was on my knees,

begging for mercy. 'You've got to see
this is more fun for you than me,

we've got to end it. I'd rather be dead.
I need you like a hole in the head.'

She flinched. I felt her draw softly away,
offended. That week was a holiday

from hurting. Now I was free of her throb
I started to act like a total slob,

ate what I liked – kebabs, very late –
watched trash on the telly, was intimate

with dubious women, didn't hear a peep
from the temples she'd left, never rested up.

But there are some things that are worse than pain.
Soon I felt totally put upon

by a zoo of symptoms, was almost dead
with their chattering inside my head

without my guardian. If you see her round
tell her I'm struggling, want to go to ground

with her for a languorous afternoon
away from myself or I'll go insane

for, though she was clothed in a tiresome ache
she cared for me, had a most healthy take

on all my excesses. She was a wife
to me. And I need her knife.

Spring

By the time we got back the street had been done
by a bunch of starlings, all of them drunk
and very abusive. I went round the block
three times to avoid them. The local tom

was out on the rampage. The precinct's trees
were growing their leaves like insects again,
a crop of locusts that all wanted in
to the butter-lit rooms. Our diaries

gave hope that the fever of spring and its wounds
would soon be over. No need to ask why
when car-alarm birds called love at the sky.
A fish like a storm cloud swallowed our moon.

Ménage à Trois

I *Body*

I sent my body to Bollywood
to become a film star. She wore only beads
draped by the see-through Ganges.

A body unchaperoned by the soul
tends to try everything – some leading men
then, bored with that, occasional women.

She acquired a habit, some discreet tattoos,
married a gangster, went on the game,
had a nervous breakdown. The shame

nearly killed her. I paid the taxi
when she came back. Neighbours strained to see.
Home is the hardest place to be.

II *Soul*

She was known round here as the woman in white
– an agoraphobic – who ordered in
all her groceries. Considered anodyne

in social circles, this spinster soul
was slowly dying of irony
like a consumption. Her attic eye

was in need of a body to make its way
down to the street – an Antarctic waste
for her, a being who was so chaste

she was abstract, couldn't even blush,
much less know the comfort of sun on her bones,
the joy of a heart attack all of her own.

III *Third Party*

But the body's unfaithful and leaves the soul
for another lover. In dishabille
before the doctors, its geometry falls

for a death that wants it, sickness and all.
The grip is erotic – it takes you down
horizontal in your dressing gown,

takes speech, takes memories and then takes breath.
Only then can you feel the humming soul
abandon its story, its particular soil

to rise like a spaceship that has locked its doors
on wondrous technology, unearthly light
which we're forced to forget once it's out of sight.

Prayer for Bandy

Just because he's dead doesn't mean
that a dog stops guarding.
And as to the question of the canine soul,
I have my opinions.

I held his breath in the palm of my hand,
fresh as a flower. Rest easy now.
He gave us our capacity
for loving him. Original sin

in dogs must be biting. Take pity on him
for being doggy, for not understanding
we don't do that here. We hope
he forgave us for killing him.

Last night, in a dream, he barked at the door.
We opened to three ethereal dogs
who ran to his basket under the stairs
and burnt there, a hearth, as we pulled on our shoes.

'One day, feeling hungry'

One day, feeling hungry, I swallowed the moon.
It stuck, like a wafer, to the top of my mouth,
dry as an aspirin. It slowly went down,

showing the gills of my vocal cords,
the folded wings in my abdomen,
the horrible twitch of my insect blood.

Lit from inside, I stood alone
(dark to myself) but could see from afar
the brightness of others who had swallowed stars.

The Pier

In memory of Joseph Brodsky
(1940-1996)

I

A poet has four bodies.
The Soviet authorities
were too late for the first,
your private polity
which, by now, had chosen democracy
and a funeral parlour
where the credit due
was given entirely to you.
You lay there, an archipelago.

Your wife had the second,
the basic note
against which poets conjugate
the intrigue between things and rhyme,
that murderous love affair with time.
Heart gave you away. Its metronome
was treacherous to you.
Now you don't, but your couplets scan:
you've left all desire to rehearse
the conjugal couplets of deep verse.
Without you, your widow lives in *vers libre*.

The third is your work.
Books perch like birds
in the palms of our open hands and feed
on our attention as we read.
We willingly give your words our breath.

The fourth is your soul.
It left you like a hawk
in search, no doubt, of other work.
Joseph, let snowflakes from its raptor cry
fall back into blankness, till the tip of a tongue
catches one of its crystals, tasting no less
than the terror of nothing more to express.

II

Even a healthy heart is lame,
limps its iambic from pillar to post,
with every ventricle pumping the same

flawed syncopation – 'I am, I am.'
Hospital tags are expensive jewellery.
Metre became the cardiogram

you lived by, words at each peak. After all,
each poet is a walk-in heart
filled with world's whooshing. Pause. Then a hall.

III

The wind on Bangor Pier draws tears
to my eyes as I tread out along each plank,
feeling my usual vertigo
at the strobe of the rucked-up tide below.

You wished me horizon in another place.
I walk out further, each lath of wood
a line of your work that will bear my weight
over the drift of the Menai Straits.

Though absent, you give me solid land.
Six planks to go and I'm out on the edge.
Stamina, you said, is a matter of style.
I find that horizon, grip it like steel.

IV

The Air's Graffiti

Stone Walls

There is an art to seeing through walls.
Old Mícheál had it, as he closed these miles

of Burren pasture. He was a man
whose straightness was in great demand

for he never saw gradient, but would build
right up a cliff face, aiming beyond

for the logical summit. He would place
two boulders together with such poise

that they'd mimic the line of a far-off spur,
rhyming with limestone, making being here

a matter of artistry. I've seen grown men
who scorn the wit of a well-placed dolmen

laugh at his corners, which made visible
the herringbone cast of his rhythmic soul,

his knowledge of water's slant disciplines.
Frost will topple a slapdash cairn

in a season. It takes a humble man to know
gaps matter more in a wall than stone,

making a window on what's really there.
A view, some people. Nothing. Air.

Woods

Midwinter and this beech wood's mind
is somewhere else. Like fallen light

snow's broken glass fills up the furrows.
Nothing that doesn't have to moves.

We walk through a frozen waterfall
of boles, all held in vertical

except for the careful woodpile laid
in pencils across a tidied glade.

Look back and from the place we were
a bird calls out because we're not there,

a double note whose range expands,
pushing the line where our racket ends

out ever further. That elaborate song
can only exist because we're gone.

A vandal, I shatter that place with a stone.
The bird is for silence. I am for home.

Red Kites at Tregaron

They know where to find me when they want to feed.
At dusk I prepare, lay out the fat

and spread unspeakable offal in snow
like scarlet necklaces. They know

how to find me. They are my words
for beauty and other birds

fight them, vulgar, down threads of air
which bring them to me. They brawl for hair,

for skin, torn giblets and gizzard which I
provide for them, domestic. Inside

the house is so cold I can see my breath,
my face in the polished oak. My mouth

is sweet with silence. Talon and claw
are tender to me, the craw

much kinder than men. What is most foul
in me kites love. At night I feel

their clear minds stirring in rowan and oak
out in the desert. I stroke

the counterpane, my sleepless skies
filled with the stars of untameable eyes.

Hermits

I know I could be really good
if I had a private loch and bog
away from the other hermits' cells.
Colman and his bloody bells

disrupt my praying. I can see
his candles burn across the bay
more hours than mine. It drives me wild,
so crowded are these blessèd isles

with would-be saints who all deny
the flesh in more outrageous ways.
I want to be indifferent as stone.
I demand to be holy all on my own.

Stone Circle

Gladulus is sad.
He stands, a menhir, misunderstood,
lichen covering him like a hood.

He mourns in dolerite. His name's
ironic. When he came,
was planted, a seed at the mercy of time,

he wanted to flower, knew that he could.
Now the surroundings have forgotten the code
to read his story. He is a lode-

stone. He knows his astronomy,
how light slants from a leaden sky
mined by the downpours. Tourists pass by

assuming that he and his circle sleep.
He suffers indignities from sheep
but throbs in the knowledge that sacred shape

has power for ever, whatever's said
from blaspheming tractors. The mad
still hear you. Gladulus, be glad.

Ancient Aunties

When Gladys put her handbag down
smack in the middle of standing stones
the dancing started. One by one

she touched the boulders, moved like a moon
from granite to sarsen, pacing out praise
for these prominent erections of man,

gliding past the North Pole of her bag
which smelt of lipstick and lavender.
Her pearls became bright satellites of her,

as she moved in ellipses, calling the gods
of darkness and chaos with parabolas
of wonder. No one can say we've gone to the dogs

while modern aunties are still in tune
with ancient eclipses, can stand alone
completing whole families of motionless stone.

The Mind Museum

I *The Museum Curator Greets the Dawn*

At nine, I switch on our TV dawn:
the South Wales Transport video game;

Treasures from our Archive (on the blink)
showing some shipwrecks before going blank;

a potted history of the mineral trade
with dotted lines across the world;

and then, my favourite, a timelapse tide
breathing water in weather-wide

and out of the harbour. And then I switch
on haulage engines for the delight

of watching the piston elbows rise and fall.
Precision makes work as musical

as any orchestra. Then I stand
on the model bridge and understand

a museum's museum is being alive.
Quiet please, madam. Yes, we close at five.

Time was they walked on water dry
so full of ships were the teeming docks.
We dream in video what they lived by day.

Masts bobbed like crosses at a crowded quay,
sank from sight inside the gurgling lock.
Time was they walked on water dry.

Men had to travel for a fireman's pay,
they sweated bullets but enjoyed the crack.
We dream in video what they lived by day.

Murmansk, Osaka, Paraguay:
the girls they met there call them back...
Time was they walked on water dry,

met Welshmen everywhere, and lay
by stanchions up some Godforsaken creeks.
We dream in video what they lived by day.

Back home in Cardiff, hear the halyards play
sweet music when the winds fall slack.
Time was they walked on water dry.
We dream in video what they lived by day.

III *Website Future*

No need for me once we're on the net,
are a wave to be surfed on, have gone world-wide.
No awkward engines to curate
but templates which never knew a tide.

And if TV signals are never lost
but flare round the world until a mind
receives them, then surely this e-mail will last
much longer than paper. Fast-forward, rewind

are history. Let the servers serve
their megabyte karma in encoded air.
Long live the roll of the mouse, the curve
of choices made when I won't be here.

Then nobody'll tell us where we've just been
but we'll make our own history, piece by piece,
be free to improvise and glean
our version, far from chronicle police.

But on monitors the bands of rain
sweep in, interference on our charts.
Remember the real matters more than the known.
Unforecast snow falls softly in our hearts.

IV *Communications*

I phoned him from a standing stone
to prove to him that I was still there.
And I was worshipful:
granite, horizon, message, air.

I called him from a holy well
hoping for miracles, a cure.
My prayers cost dearly in time
and candles. But he didn't care.

I dialled via satellite.
I needed an answer to my despair.
I got it. *Sorry, we can't connect you.*
Please try again later. Nobody here.

V *On Duty*

First things first: the Crossword of the Day,
which I do while showing visitors the way.

I'm paid for boredom and the tide
of non-events on which I ride.

We're waiting to hear about our jobs.
Six across could be the *Ace of Spades.*

What would I curate if I had to leave?
These mud flats? *Anagram: Reprieve.*

The open handbag of a screaming gull?
The passing clouds? *Fifteen is Dull.*

The crossword setter, my anonymous friend
gives me clues to my unknown mind.

These are snakes and ladders you'll never climb
or follow to anywhere. Last word is *Time.*

VI *Night Galleries*

Maybe today they'll change the tapes!
It's the same old stories – first there was steam,
steel, then depression, then developed bay –
stories so fixed I can never say
more than they let me. At night I dream

these galleries shift. We open screens,
show new exhibits. The best one's my heart
in a glass case and it switches on
and off like a light bulb. This intimate room
is floodlit, is a work of art. Stop, start. Stop, start. Stop, start.

Will and the Wall

'Well!' said Will to the wall,
but the wall said nothing at all to Will.

*

'Forsooth!' The Count of Monte Cristo eyed his cell
with calculation. He'd heard the tapping,
had decided escape was a matter of style

and special attention. No mortar could withstand his stare.
Nothing would love him as much again
as the wall he seduced, that became his door.

*

When pushed, the wall said 'Nothing' to Will
who, shocked, could only manage a 'Well!'

*

Kerrunch! Now *that's* talking.
A cartoon cat
is a concertina played by a fall
and hitting top C. It's broom-handle
heart attack, *yoiks!* and *kerpow!*
It's saying: fantasy's all very well,
you may *think* you're an arrow
but a wall's in the way
and the literal's stronger, remember.
Splatt! Now.

*

Once it had started to talk, the wall
couldn't stop itself. Will listened well.

*

And overnight these words appeared
in day-glo spray paint:
          PC Evans is a sad man.
          PC Davies needs a vasectomy
and this on the station. Now I know
I'm just a cleaner, but stones cry out
their truthfulness. I'm paid
to hush them. Best thing is, my fee
doesn't cover insistence. See, the next day
it's *Evans* who *needs a vasectomy*
and *D. is a pansy.*
Nothing at all to do with me,
but there's gold in them graffiti.

*

In winter the crack let in the slugs
and sky to the kitchen. The garden looked lush
through the chink, less slum
than tropical. Mysterious glair
jazzed up the carpets. The slugs themselves,
of course, were never there.

*

Well, thingummy, thingummy Will tum wall.
Ti tum wall thingummy thingummy Will.

*

Been swimming so long this water's a wall
that I can see through.
Kick, tumble turn and breathe,
pulling so fast that I'm standing still.
Repeat it all as before and turn.
Bricked up inside this barricade
I'm climbing swiftly on liquid ropes
but going nowhere. Don't look down
in case I remember the air and drown.

*

And it was well between Will and the wall,
so we all came to sit and stare with Will.

*

When I die I shall bequeath a wall
to this village so the kids with their balls
can do rebound practice. What else is there to do
out in the country? I'll site it carefully,
away from the houses, so the structure can ring
with ricochet, swoop, reverse catch and swing
and kids will play on when the adults' eyes
have lost sight of the grid for which they aim
on summer evenings. In time their game
will become its own end and, piece by piece,
will dismantle the inner carapace
that has kept their souls from the wider view
not behind my memorial wall but through
its structure. Balls bounce back
at predictable angles, thoughts recoil
at the barricade's blankness, an inner door
swings open. All you have to do is stare
for long enough and everything's there.

The Flaggy Shore
(for Nora Nolan)

Even before I've left, I long
for this place. For hay brought in before the rain,
its stooks like stanzas, for glossy cormorants
that make metal eyes and dive like hooks,
fastening the bodice of the folding tide
which unravels in gardens of carraigín.
I walk with the ladies who throw stones at the surge
and their problems, don't answer the phone
in the ringing kiosk. Look. In the clouds
hang pewter promontories, long bays
whose wind-indented silent coasts
make me homesick for where I've not been.
Quicksilver headlands shoot into the night
till distance and the dying of day
dull steel and vermilion to simple lead
blown downwind to the dark, then out of sight.

KEEPING MUM

(2003)

PREFACE

I live a double life. I was brought up speaking a language which predates the Roman invasion of Britain. When I'm frightened I swear in ancient Brythonic idioms. Yet I'm a city dweller, and surf the net using the language of the Saxons who pushed the Welsh into the hills of western Britain in the sixth century. I write in both languages. It's a difficult domestic arrangement, but it holds.

One of my survival tactics until now has been to keep both sides of my linguistic family apart for as long as possible. I publish one book in Welsh, the next in English. Translating my own work from Welsh into English has held little appeal, simply because the audience and concerns addressed are distinct and, often, mutually antagonistic. Also, I dislike repeating myself.

The death of the Welsh language has been predicted for many centuries. With devolution some political optimists declared that the battle for the language had been won. I disagree, having seen my grandparents' village changing from being virtually monoglot Welsh to being a rural community which will have more in common with the Lake District or the Yorkshire Dales than with its own past in the Cambrian mountains. If the language is dying it seems important to know who or what killed it.

In 1999 I wrote a book-length detective story investigating the murder of my mother tongue, calling it *Y Llofrudd Iaith*, 'The Language Murderer'. The plot of the original book was set in a West Wales village, where an old lady, my embodiment of the Welsh language, had been found dead. In the book as a whole I wanted to explore how we could free ourselves of the idea of a "mother tongue" with all its accompanying psychological baggage and its infantilising of native speakers. Detective Carma, half-Welsh, half-Japanese, was the investigating officer and I'm not going to tell you the outcome.

Can you imagine having to speak Spanish for the rest of your life because everybody else around you has stopped speaking English at home? The prospect of losing a whole culture is an existential nightmare for a Welsh-speaker, fraught with questions of one's own responsibility in preserving collective values without becoming a parrot for the past. To most English speakers, it can't seem any more important than the loss of Morris dancing. I was persuaded, however, that the fate of a language might be of interest to those concerned with the wider linguistic ecology – after all, if endangered plants offer cures for cancer, what essential directions might be hidden in obscure Welsh proverbs about never ploughing at a run?

The first section of *Keeping Mum* represents as much of *The Language Murderer* as I was able to translate in a fairly direct fashion. Only a handful of the poems are literal versions. Richard Poole translated 'Her End' in consultation with me. Revisiting the subject stimulated entirely new poems in English, and I allowed those to take shape. These are translations without an original text – perhaps a useful definition of poetry.

Section two of this book is a more radical recasting of my original detective story and a meditation on mental illness and language. In his essay on poetry and psychoanalysis in *Promises, Promises*, Adam Phillips quotes Lacan echoing Freud: 'Psychoanalysis should be the science of language inhabited by the subject. From the Freudian point of view man is the subject captured and tortured by language.' My translated detective was to be a psychiatrist in a mental hospital, investigating how abuses of language had led to his patients' illnesses.

Therapy's based on the premise that an accurate description of a situation releases the patient from being neurotically bound to it. Psychoanalysts have even more faith in language than do poets. In the face of experience our explanations always break down. Far from being a failure, however, this wordlessness is usually a clue that something more truthful than our own account of the world is being approached: the 'keeping mum' of this book's title.

The third section of the book, *Chaotic Angels*, looks at communications between different realms of awareness. Commissioned by Kathryn McDowell, Director of the City of London Festival for the Angel Series of concerts in 2002, the sonnets were written to match Dragan Andjelic's canvases exhibited in the Wren churches of the City. They focus on angels as messengers from another realm. I use the language of modern Chaos Theory to re-imagine angels as part of our everyday lives – at the centre of experiences like depression and bereavement.

Detective, psychiatrist, angel – the sequence of communicators leads out ever further, in the service of a clarity which is not my own.

I

The Language Murderer

POLICE FILE

A Poet's Confession

'I did it. I killed my mother tongue.
I shouldn't have left her
there on her own.
All I wanted was a bit of fun
with another body
but now that she's gone –
it's a terrible silence.

She was highly strung,
quite possibly jealous.
After all, I'm young
and she, the beauty,
had become a crone
despite all the surgery.

Could I have saved her?
made her feel at home?

Without her reproaches.
I feel so numb,
not free, as I'd thought...

Tell my lawyer to come.
Until he's with me,
I'm keeping mum.'

What's in a Name?

Today the wagtail finally forgot
that I once called it *sigl-di-gwt*.

It didn't give a tinker's toss,
kept right on rooting in river moss,

(no longer *mwswgl*) relieved, perhaps,
that someone would be noticing less

about its habits. Magpies' fear of men
lessened, as we'd lost one means

(the word *pioden*) of keeping track
of terrorist birds out in the back.

Lleian wen is not the same as 'smew'
because it's another point of view,

another bird. There's been a cull:
gwylan's gone and we're left with 'gull'

and blunter senses till that day
when 'swallows', like *gwennol*, might stay away.

Mother Tongue

'I started to translate in seventy-three
in the schoolyard. For a bit of fun
to begin with – the occasional "fuck"
for the bite of another language's smoke
at the back of my throat, its bitter chemicals.
Soon I was hooked on whole sentences
behind the shed, and lessons in Welsh
seemed very boring. I started on print,
Jeeves & Wooster, Dick Francis, James Bond,
in Welsh covers. That worked for a while
until Mam discovered Jean Plaidy inside
a Welsh concordance one Sunday night.
There were ructions: a language, she screamed,
should be for a lifetime. Too late for me.
Soon I was snorting Simenon
and Flaubert. Had to read much more
for any effect. One night I OD'd
after reading far too much Proust.
I came to, but it scared me. For a while
I went Welsh-only but it was bland
and my taste was changing. Before too long
I was back on translating, found that three
languages weren't enough. The "ch"
in German was easy, Rilke a buzz...
For a language fetishist like me
sex is part of the problem. Umlauts make me sweat,
so I need a multilingual man
but they're rare in West Wales and tend to be
married already. If only I'd kept
myself much purer, with simpler tastes,
the Welsh might be living...
                              Detective, you speak
Russian, I hear, and Japanese.
Could you whisper some softly?
I'm begging you. Please...'

Farm Visit

Each cow has a hairstyle
and walks in high heels,
bearing a handbag – the reticulum,
in which she transports her chewing gum.

They lick their nostrils
with liquorish tongues.
'You like that, detective? Never turn
your back on a cow or assume she's tame.

My mother was trampled,
had to be pulled
free from the herd.' The kodak field
was suddenly filled

with black and white Holsteins
like standing stones
around us, their sileage breath
sweet, oppressive. 'Your sister confessed...'

'This village had already died.
One prion, detective, has killed a trade:
the butcher wielding his favourite knife,
a food chain. A language. A way of life.'

Suddenly a restless cow reared,
starting a huffing stampede
towards us. Shouting, the farmer tore
a heifer aside by her jigsaw ear,

and, holding me roughly by the hand,
showed me how to stand my ground.
We played musical statues with the herd,
which froze every time he uttered a word.

Home Cooking

'I thought she was magic. Like the time
we went to pick *llysiau duon bach*
up on the mountain. I rolled the fruit
carefully between finger and thumb,
pleased with the patina that made them look
like mineral berries sweated out
of bitter bedrock. I heard a shout

and my mother said she'd see us back
at the house. We were ling-di-long,
stopped at the quarry to throw stones...
When we got in, a cooling rack
held two steaming pies, the washing-up done.
I was stunned and couldn't work out
how her time had gone slower. 'Short cut,'

they told me. But a lift
was the real answer. Then I knew
that mothers didn't live in straight lines.
Her world was folded, she had a gift
for swiftness, sweetness and for telling lies.
My faith in directness was undermined.
I was always the plodder, a long way behind.'

llysiau duon bach: bilberries

150

Small Holding

Last light on the hilltops and his crop of stones
is ripening nicely. It's time he trashed
my grandfather's hedgerows of beech,
pleached them against the rustling rain.
'I haven't been down to the village again

since the night of the concert. I keep
myself to myself. I take it you've heard
the rumours of big cats hunting sheep.
Ask about killing the already dead
and the beast of prey inside the head.'

'My father was distant...'

'Faced with perpetual winter in the house
he turned his attention, the greater part of love,
outside and kept a daily Weather Book,
an act of faith that things were on the move,
despair can change. His neat Remarks

show him a connoisseur of Wet
in months so boring I suspect a code
in "Fair but rather sultry in the E",
and "Wintry showers", outlined in red.
The highlight is: "A cloudburst in Cwmdu,

extensive damage caused." It's plain –
a light, then gentler, later stiffening breeze,
a week in July of "very BRIGHT".
No comments then for several days.
He was an adulterer with light.'

A Past

Don't look. But see that mountain there?
I've had sex with her often.
Now we're only friends
but, God, I was very fond of her,

spent many an active afternoon
in her secret crannies,
hiking, sweating.
She liked me alone,

wouldn't tolerate company
(a jealous mountain).
I once took a gang
to see her, but she'd have none of me

pulled up her B roads, made a mist
to hide herself from us.
We ended up
stuck in a farmer's ditch. What a bitch!

Her End

'The end was dreadful. Inside a dam burst
and blood was everywhere. Out of her mouth
came torrents of words, *da yw dant*
i atal tafod, gogoniannau'r Tad
in scarlet flowers – *yn Abercuawg*
yd ganant gogau – the blood was black,
full of filth, a well that amazed
with its vivid idioms – *bola'n holi ble mae 'ngheg?* –
and always fertile, *yes no pwdin llo,*
and psalms were gathering in her viscera
and gushing out of her, proverbs, coined words,
the names of plants, seven types of gnat,
dragonfly, rosemary, mountain ash,
then disgusting pus, and long-lost terms
like *gwelltor* and *rhychor*, her vomit a road
leading away from her, a force
leaving the fortress of her breath,
gwyr a aeth Gatráeth.
And after the crisis, nothing to be done
but watch her die, as saliva and sweat
of words poured out like ants – *padell pen-glin,*
Anghydffurfiaeth, clefyd y paill,
and, in spite of our efforts, in the grey of dawn
the haemorrhage ended, her lips were white,
the odd drop splashing. Then she was gone.'

Da yw dant i atal tafod: A tooth is a good barrier for the tongue; *gogoniannau'r Tad*: the Father's glories; *yn abercuawg yd ganant gogau:* cuckoos sing in Abercuawg (from a 9th-century poem); *bola'n holi, ble mae 'ngheg*: my stomach asking where my mouth is; *yes no pwdin llo*: yes, no, calf's pudding (referring to the rich milk given by a cow who's just given birth); *gwelltor* and *rhychor*: the left- and right-hand oxen in a ploughing pair; *gwyr a aeth Gatráeth*: men went to Catraeth (from Aneirin's 6th-century poem, *Y Gododdin*); *padell pen-glin:* knee-cap; *Anghydffurfiaeth*: Nonconformity; *clefyd y paill:* hay fever.

Aphasia

I ask for 'hammer' but am given 'spade',
feel like some 'tea' but order 'orangeade'

by mistake. I specify 'velvet' but am given 'silk'
in a colour I don't even like

but I take it, pretend. Someone's cut the string
between each word and its matching thing,

so my mind's a junk shop of where I've been.
I'll never know now what I really mean.

Brainstorming

What if I slept tonight beside Taliesin's stone
to solve the murder? Would it send me mad,
or make me a poet? It must be remade

daily, this moorland, as it is destroyed
each time we leave it. See it shake
with wind that knocks the noisy larks

off their high pillars. Even they fall
in silence. I need to know
what survives forgetting. The shadow

grown here but never harvested?
The hillside's humming? I could pray
to know this tumultuous energy

before it falls into pools, then streams
down to the valley into livestock, names,
marriages, murders and on into time.

Forget forgetting. Will I survive
the lichen hissing like flying spray,
the mountain wave under me giving way?

Taliesin: the 6th-century poet who later became a mythical figure and shape-shifter. His stone, in Cardiganshire, is reputed either to drive people who sleep there mad or turn them into poets.

II

Keeping Mum

MEMOIRS OF
A PSYCHIATRIST

Lifesaving for Psychiatrists

Of course, it's violent. The apparently drowned
have a grip that's deadly. To master a man,
practise the different breaks on dry land;

bring up your knee to his groin;
on his throat you can use your palms,
or press his eyeballs in with your thumbs

till you're the master. It looks like sex
or a tango. Gaining the upper hand
in water is beautiful and reminds

the cultured observer of Beatrice
and Dante floating in Paradise,
buoyant and easy. Face to face

with a drowned man, never promise
that you can save him.
That depends on the kiss.

Consultant

I am the one who makes the statues move,
who teaches the dead to rise and love

again, more wisely. I help the damned
explore what happened, who condemned

them each to their particular hell.
Yes, I'm in favour of using pills,

but my main job is to translate
pain into tales they can tolerate

in another language. We've pleasant grounds.
Care to come with me on my rounds?

Dissociation

CASE TAPES
Miss D

'On the pavilion
rain's small hands
tap braille on the windows.
I don't understand:

Someone was killed here,
but no one will tell.
I watch as patients
play games of bowls,

rolling wood planets
under sighing trees.
That corpse I mentioned?
I think it's me.'

Early Days in Psychiatry

Before the arrival of modern medicines
patients were frozen like statuary,
condemned to act the seven deadly sins
in tableaux of torment. We set some free

with lithium (remember Lot's wife?
her salt helps the heavy).
Even the barbarous ECT
seemed like a miracle. Rural life

was a nightmare. We'd find
children kept in chicken sheds
rocking like roosters, out of their minds
with neglect. A boy, half dead,

chained like a dog. Although we freed
his body, we never touched the fear
that held him – a stronger, invisible lead –
to that stinking farmyard. We'd hear

whispers of incest and often see
moon faces in windows, hurriedly withdrawn.
But I learned their code of secrecy,
listened at hedges and prescribed to thorns.

Finding the Bodies

DREAM WORK
Miss D

'Last night I dug up my father's vegetable patch
in Bridge Street, by the old swing.
"You always have to dig in the end,
I've put this off for far too long,"
I said to myself. The dead
– no, the murdered – are given a tent
where their body's located, an official camp
for the start of enquiries. I made a note
to tell the shrink that an underground stream
ran from left to right across the plot.
"We'll have asparagus from that," I thought.'

Tongue Fetishist

I've had two Christs already this year
one Hitler and a Mother of God
in our private clinic. I spend my time
listening to them, making things clear,
pointing to any suggestive rhymes

that might lead to reason.
Sense almost always follows sound,
so I've found. I speak
six languages, so keeping mum
isn't an option, but I'm a freak...

That book is my *Atlas of the Tongue*,
shows you diseases of the mouth,
fungus and tumours, how to take care
of the flesh for talking. Yours, my dear,
is remarkable. Come closer. Say Aah...

A Teenage Craze

CASE TAPES
Miss D

'Curious, one day, about the other side,
I made friends with an "Englie" behind the shed.

Like "Welshies", they played by the railway track,
counted coal trucks as they passed

until we were giddy. Then we picked
sticky honeysuckle bracts

and she showed me how to pinch and pull
the flower's filament through its style

and place the nectar drop on my tongue,
a vaccine for sweetness. It all came undone

for no reason in the toilets one day
when the game turned into strangling me

for treason. I didn't think to resist
as the walls went screechy. I tasted rust

from the fire in my gullet, because I knew
it wasn't personal, but a clue

to the trap that was sprung inside my throat
just waiting to catch me. So I kept

my eyes wide open, though my vision bruised,
and I watched as I died, mildly amused

by the fear in my murderer's eyes. That grew
till the monoglot girl had to let me go

because her nerve failed her. I was nearly dead.
But I was the one with the rush to the head.'

Therapy

Did you hear the one about the shrink
who let obsessive-compulsives clean his house
as if their illnesses were his?
They made good caretakers, stayed up all night
rattling doorknobs, testing locks,
domesticated poltergeists.

He started an amateur dramatics group
with the psychotics, who had a ball
in togas, till they burnt down the hall.
Chronic depressives are always apart,
so he'd check them through his telescope,
placed them in poses from classical art

and, of course, they'd hardly ever move,
added a certain style to the grounds.
He recorded Tourette patients' sounds,
sold them to pop groups as backing tracks.
Whenever possible, he'd encourage love
between staff and patients. He had a knack

with manics, whom he sent out to shop
for all his parties, gave tarot cards
to schizoids so they could read their stars.
Perhaps he was flip with other people's pain
but his patients loved him and his hope
that two or three madnesses might make one sane.

A Promising Breakthrough

CASE TAPES
Miss D

'You're right, I don't remember the egg
before it was broken. When it was whole,
as a word it filled my six-year-old palms,
oblong, complete and a little warm,
a gift for my mother. I recall the jolt –
a blue hydrangea as I bit my tongue –
pain in my marrow, not having hands
free to protect myself. The dog
came to lick up the horrible yolk
that oozed from my fingers, a shocking glue,
from the jagged jigsaw of shell.' Long pause. 'I felt
it was me who was broken because all my care
couldn't save my treasure'. Even longer spell.
'Egg doesn't always mean preciousness.
It was still an egg when it was a mess.'
'Oh God. Don't tell me. A lifetime's sense of loss
based on mistranslation?' 'That's entirely poss.'

Spread a Little Happiness

Now that millions are taking the pills
and pissing out Prozac, the salmon trout
are very much mellower and rivers run
with chemical happiness. My gift
to mosquitos is a blast of 'cool
head' that just takes the edge
off problems like dying. Mozzie, take a hit
of anti-depressant. I recommend it!

A Talent for Fainting

'First time I fainted I'd just told a lie
to the boy next door who'd come to play.
I'd said my name was Jenny.
It's not. I found a living bird
being eaten by ants. It sounds absurd,
but I quite like falling. They gave me pills
but that never stopped me, I could faint at will
fall gracefully, and always ended up draped
round someone compliant. There was a man
who said he was married to me and slept
in my bed. I don't recollect
a wedding but he was always kind
and good at catching. Where did I go
when my awareness left my mind?
Haven't the faintest. But I seem too old
for a woman who's barely lived a week
in twenty-six years. Doctor, how dare
you suggest it's a reaction to fear.
Whatever's wrong is much more rare
than common terror. Quickly, call
for someone stronger. I'm going to fall...'

Psychiatist, Twitcher

Words always return to the scene of the crime.
They have a legitimate point of view.
And I have mine.

You have to be patient, because speech is shy,
won't come if you're noisy,
or keep asking why.

I use my silence as a khaki hide
to flush out the wildlife.
I make tea inside,

have a textbook wish-list, hope for the rare
so I can tick it,
prove it was there.

Sometimes I catch the glint of an eye
in my binoculars –
in here, with me.

What is this presence that dares give chase
and me, a doctor?
My most dangerous case.

A Question

'Doctor, do you think you can lose your soul?'
Miss D once asked me. I tried to stay cool
but the question shook me. 'I dreamt I was in hell,'
the patient continued, ignoring the dread
on my face. 'Although I was dead
my body continued, couldn't disappear
from the life of the living. Loved ones tore
my organs daily, unaware
that they broke my body by walking the streets.
At one point I became liquid dirt,
spattered and macerated into an ooze
a molecule thin but I couldn't lose
my consciousness. I felt everything:
the whole world tasted of nothing but shit,
I was shit incarnate because I felt it
in every particle of what had been me.
And I was a torturer too, for the guilty
had to hurt others – I was assigned
"soft duties" – hammering living bones
"till they stung but didn't ulcerate,"
said Quality Control. Rodin's Gates
of Hell were there, covered in gore,
and you had to look at them. There was more...
Doctor,' she asked again, 'can lose your soul?'

I'm not religious. Her despair
appalled me. Then I didn't dare
say 'Yes'. But knowing what I know now
I wish to God that I hadn't said 'No'.

Panic Attack

You've fallen through ice. Above you men
with ladders are sidling to where you fell in

to this cold cathedral with its shattered dome.
Ice has you in its picture frame

for a full-length portrait but minus breath.
Light doesn't help. Safety's underneath,

a little deeper, if only you dare
look up to the jagged dark. That's air,

shouts, dogs barking, warm hands and ropes.
Aim for the dark. It's your only hope.

Seaside Sanatorium

CASE TAPES
Miss D

'I live at a distance
from my own life,
a true provincial. That delay
has cost me everything.

Dogs search, frantic, for the thread
by which to unravel a slackening tide.
They never find it.

The ocean's a bore
with its circular breathing.
Light, also boring, moves up a gear
and a thrush cries "Cricket, wicket,"
everything twice.

"Start living," they say,
but I don't know how.
My life is a party
in another room
and I'm not invited.
I like my own gloom.

The nurses push you
to walk outside.
I prefer the skies
inside my head.

They'll all be sorry
when they find me dead.'

Night Passage to Nantucket

Those days night ferries travelled blind
and, once they were over Nantucket Bar,
used a single searchlight to pick out buoys
and find the channel. I sat outside,
watched the light swinging as if it could feel
the port side cans and starboard cones,
reading the fairway by floodlit braille.

My patients fumble for every word.
I refuse them the searchlight, sit on my hands
as they drift towards their most dangerous sands.
I must stay quiet. They have to learn
to distrust car headlights, that a landing star
is a plane. They need new marks
for self-navigation, to know where they are.

The Perfect Crime

CASE TAPES
Miss D

He killed her from fifteen years ago,
the perfect murder, with her own hands
and his suggestions about what she should be.
This poem doesn't rhyme but it's true.

It was a psychic slaying. His alibi
was watertight, he was already dead,
had left no fingerprints but lies –
all she wanted was to rhyme with him.

A delayed reaction meant that she took years
to see his meaning when he'd cut the ground
from under any of her future feet.
This poem isn't true but rhymes.

And then she got it: that she had no self
because she'd depended on his 'you',
and that was gone. She had to die.
This poem rhymes and is also true.

Retired Psychiatrist

Youngsters today don't speak semaphore
or even learn basic Morse Code any more.

The lightships are gone,
and their besweatered men

who watched seas for me. I used to know
where the occulting word-buoys were moored

but somebody's moved them – saboteurs
or my latest stroke. There is a tear

in the rip tide and I hear the roar
of the shoal that will wreck me, it's very near.

Across this estuary of lightest airs
others have hoisted spinnakers

of unearthly beauty and, silently,
glide out, like me, to the open sea.

Memorial Service
Miss D

Nothing anyone ever said helped.
She took up hobbies and even tried
to break with her mother, though she was dead.

For a while it seemed to be going so well.
She was optimistic, phoned me to tell
that she loved her courses. She was so frail

but no one can give their strength away
to carry another. Nothing I'd say
made any difference. At the end of the day

she just got tired. Hope takes work
and is exhausting. She drew a blank.
What chances have we if this girl sank?

What They Don't Teach You in Medical School

Guilt feels like love but never is.
Love feels like boredom because it's a home;
it offers excitement but mainly rest.
Ego's flamingo, but the common herd
is where your patients – even the best –
belong. Accusation's a front
for self-aggression. Help patients hunt
their monsters – make sure they're never your own –
to their shit-covered lairs. Beware
of omniscience, it makes a fool
of every psychiatrist. Play Virgil
to Dante as he walks through hell
then let him decide if he wants to be well.
You are the pagan who's outside the walls
of their paradise. You must bow your head
when you hear your Dante torn to shreds
by gods not your own. Many say no
to heaven. You must let them go.

III

Chaotic Angels

1 Pagan Angel

You ask me how it is we know
God's talking, not us. When even a stone
can photograph lilies and, as it falls,
prove that gravity's no more than speed?
When loquacious skies call
in gamma-rays, radio, infra-red,
and that's if we're not listening at all?

The heart's a chamber whose broody dead
stage pagan rituals. Wind blows
across stone lintels, making a tune
about absent bodies.
You ask me again:
'Where's the angel acoustic?'
My dear, the curlew. The quickening rain.

2 Tarot Angel

You can chase him through the Tarot de Marseilles.
Here is the Tower with its tumbling men
and crashing illusions. Take great care
as you decide what this all might mean:
that's His department. After all, we're scared
of the Death card and the Hanging Man
though what they signify is far from clear.

It has to be lived. Of course, we all die
but we live as though this weren't possible.
Who says this is folly? It might come true.
Step over the cliff with me, the Fool,
take a chance on changing. Die every day
as if you were living and that you knew
that broad roads score the blazing sky.

3 Fire Angel

For now it's music that holds up this church –
chromatic buttresses, a spandrel wall
of finest vibrato, while the spire
narrows to nothing on its rising scale,
leaving the weathercock to turn at will,
prompted by any weathery whim.
Melody, for once, has overcome fire.

But I've seen different. Led by a boy
who lit up plastic-bottle flares
and guided me, nervous, underground
in Acco, knowing that I should feel fear,
but I didn't and he led me far
into flickering vaults, a garrison
built by crusaders, remembered in flame.

4 Angels of Stage and Screen

Every actor in Hollywood knows
you have to keep still.
Don't wobble your head when talking to girls.
You let the action come to you.
Cultivate your charisma too,
mortify flesh in the latest gym.
These are the ways to become a star.

Angels are opposite. A modern kind
appears on radar, so sailors see
much deeper than distance. No 'Me, Me, Me',
these are messages without a source,
at least, to our knowledge. A crew stands awed,
surrounded by angel anomalies
dancing, invisible, on a flat-calm sea.

5 Minimal Angel

The smallest angel of which we're aware
is a 'spinning nothing'. Angel of dust,
angel of stem cells, of pollen grains,
angel of branches which divide to a blur
as they're ready to bud, becoming more
than their sum was even an hour before.
Angel of dog smells, angels of stairs,

of gardening, marriage. Cherubim
of rotting rubbish, of seeing far,
of rain's paste diamonds after a shower.
Radiation angels, angels of mud,
angels of slowing and of changing gear,
angels of roundabouts, and of being here
all say: 'You were made for this – prayer.'

6 Angel of Depression

Why would an angel choose to come here
if it weren't important? Into stuffy rooms
smelling of cabbage? Into the tedium of time,
which weighs like gravity on any messenger
used to more freedom and who has to wear
a dingy costume, so as not to scare
the humans. Wouldn't even an angel despair?

Don't say it's an honour to have fought
with depression's angel. It always wears
the face of my loved ones as it tears
the breath from my solar plexus, grinds
my face in the ever-resilient dirt.
Oh yes, I'm broken but my limp
is the best part of me. And the way I hurt.

7 How to Read Angels

Yes, information, but that's never all,
there's some service, a message. A lie dispelled,
something forgiven, an alternative world
glimpsed, for a moment, what you wanted to hear
but never thought possible. You feel a fool
but do something anyway and are filled
with delight as you unfold

like a wing in a thermal. If it's peace
you're left with after your left-of-field
encounter, that's angels. If you feel less fear
and trust yourself less. But beware
of other voices, easier to bear
which sound more like angels than angels do
but leave you in turmoil, saying 'More. More. More.'

8 In Memory of Katherine James
Killed September 11, 2001

You can believe that God exists
but the devil's a way of talking. Yes,
except that demons are us in disguise
as angel voices. They never surprise
but confirm our hatreds. We easily miss
that they're nonsense messages, an excuse
to megaphone the ego's madness.

She was a musician, so was used
to leaving her body and strolling through
the wide avenues and sunny porticoes
that melody built. She had an ear
for what was beyond herself, was more
than her wishes. Therefore, I hear
her lovely harmonics in that terrible roar.

9 Angel of Dying

'A young boy dying on a ward in Kabul
wouldn't stop singing – made music from screams,
wouldn't sleep, wouldn't drink, but chanted dreams
in ferocious head notes. He frightened us all
but held his dying like a torch of flame
for us to follow. Arches leapt darkly overhead,
threw shadows over us. He led

on past comfort, past reason or blame
with the terrible energy of the dead
whose death is more life than flesh can bear,
a birth, not an ending. This truth tore
the living to pieces. Then silence sang of him instead...
I've never forgotten him. No, don't ask
about dying. How to live is the task.'

10 Angel of Healing

Every disease is a work of art
if you play it rightly. Of course, it hurts
like hell, but can be used
as a reminder that your mind
is not on its business, which is 'now',
however painful. Novalis knew
that all illness requires a musical cure.

By this he meant: whatever the form
imposed by arthritis, or by the gout,
your job's to compose yourself round about
its formal restrictions, and make that sing,
even to death. And all that pain?
Messengers from your beloved to say
'Wait for me, darling, I'm on my way!'

11 The Good, the Bad and the Complex

In angel orders there are twelve degrees
of chaos. Nonsense; then scramble;
raving that's modified into scat.
The sleeping orders' psychedelic dreams
give rise to cities, till they wake
and trigger a local apocalypse.
There are angels of breakdown, and collapse

is their specialist subject. Angels of decline,
angels of entropy. Then angels who tell
you what to do when (that's close to hell);
angels pedantic, angels of the Law.
The Complex orders know what chaos is for –
that's self-forgetting – and, greatest of all,
is the Angel of Not Knowing a Thing Any More.

12 Christ as Angel of the Will of God

What would it be to move beyond
our need for angels? Just to relax
might take us a century. To like
that sensation, longer. We'd understand
and calculate the logarithms of grace
to easy solutions in our sleep.
Not to need messages about
but to be, instead, a literal place

we have a map for? Because it's here:
a murderous waste ground. To be free
to gather bouquets of nettles? to be
those passionate kisses? that hot pain?
Not to mind hurting because you see
Christ bringing cool dock leaves of mercy.

Printed in the USA
CPSIA information can be obtained
at www.ICGtesting.com
JSHW012030140824
68134JS00033B/2982

9 781852 247232